Contents

William Rocke is a journalist with *The Sunday Press* in Dublin, where he is Assistant News Editor and also contributes a weekly showbiz column. He is the author of *Operation Birdie* and has also written plays including 'Try Anything Twice' and 'Family Affairs'.

WILLIAM ROCKE

BLACKWATER PRESS

Cover photo: Argentina's Diego Maradona scores his famous 'Hand of God' goal against England in the quarter-final of the 1986 World Cup in Mexico. *(Popperfoto)*

Printed in Ireland at the press of the publishers

Broomhill Road,
Tallaght,
Dublin 24.

ISBN 0 86121 508 7

Editor
Anna O'Donovan

Design & Layout
M & J Graphics Ltd.

Front Cover
Philip Ryan

Foreword

World Cup Wonders is one of those engrossing books you begin to read and find it difficult to put down. When I received the original proof copy from the publisher I gave it a cursory glance – then found myself hooked. I finished it in two sessions.

In this era of satellite television, today's generation would be excused for thinking that the World Cup gripped the globe from the outset. Not so, as the author reminds us in the first chapter of his book. Although Jules Rimet, the man who conceived soccer's greatest tournament, was always going to be on a winner, his vision which now rivals the Olympic Games as a sporting spectacle, did have a rather humble beginning in Uruguay in 1930.

I first became fascinated with the World Cup when, as a starry-eyed schoolboy player of 13 in 1954, myself and my team-mates thrilled to the skills of Puskas, Hidegkuti and Bozsik in the great Hungarian team of that era. Marvellous to meet them again in *World Cup Wonders*!

It's every player's ambition to play for his country in the World Cup. Unfortunately, I missed out; in my era the Irish squad was not quite as well organised as it is today. The nearest I came to getting there was in 1966 when Spain beat us 1-0 in a play-off in Paris.

Reading *World Cup Wonders* brought back a lot of memories. Great players, great occasions, the occasional riot. The author has captured the magic of a great sporting event down through the years. I have no hesitation in recommending it to soccer fans everywhere.

John Giles.

John Giles, multi-capped Irish international, player/manager of Ireland 1974-80. He is now a respected match television commentator.

(The fee for this foreword has kindly been donated to charity.)

· THE FIRST WORLD CUP ·

THE sedate Frenchman sitting among the other VIPs in the packed stadium in Montevideo in Uruguay was a proud man. It was the summer of 1930 and Jules Rimet, president of the French Football Federation, was about to see a project he had worked on for years come to fruition – the final of the first World Cup soccer tournament. In recognition of Monsieur Rimet's endeavour, a trophy had been named in his honour.

Both himself and colleague Henri Delaunay had sought for years to set up a tournament which they hoped would unite, in peaceful combat, the soccer nations of the globe. Now the first World Cup was about to be brought to a successful conclusion.

The two teams which had battled their way to the first World Cup final were Uruguay, the tournament hosts, and their long-time rivals, Argentina. Looking around at the 95,000 excited fans jammed into the Centenario Stadium, especially built for the occasion, Monsieur Rimet may have been slightly apprehensive about his plan for a World Cup for soccer nations.

Uruguay and Argentina were so anxious to have their names inscribed on the Jules Rimet trophy as World Cup champions that they were prepared to do battle for the honour both on and off the field. For days preceding the final there had been riots and heated arguments on the streets of cities throughout Uruguay and Argentina. In Buenos Aires, thousands of fanatical Argentinian soccer fans, unable to get accommodation on the fleet of ships leaving for Montevideo, had stormed around the city shooting off fireworks, and occasionally guns, in frustration.

Each day the Argentinian players were escorted under heavy police guard from their hotel to their training quarters. Back home, their soccer-crazy followers were still smarting from the 2-1 defeat which the Uruguayans had inflicted on their amateur team in the soccer final of the Olympic Games two years previously.

In Montevideo, relationships between the officials in charge of both teams were less than cordial, and it looked like the game to determine who would be crowned first-ever World Cup champions would be a torrid one.

It was in 1920 that FIFA, the Federation of International Football Associations, had agreed, in principle, to hold a tournament between the soccer nations of the world. Jules Rimet was the driving force behind the project and a trophy, designed by the French sculptor Abel Lafleur, was named in his honour. It stood 12 inches high and was made of solid gold.

Unfortunately, due to the vast distances that European teams had to travel to South America, and since modes of transport were slow, a mere 13 nations answered the call to the first World Cup. The list included the USA, whose team members were a mixture of expatriates from the British Isles and others who had emigrated to Canada, and then moved to America.

Uruguay, as Olympic Games champions, had the honour of staging the tournament. Only France, Belgium, Romania and Yugoslavia crossed the Atlantic from Europe to challenge the South Americans, even though the host nation had guaranteed to pay all expenses. King Carol of Romania at least showed some enthusiasm – he picked his national team and ordered that they be given adequate time off to train.

The 13 teams were split into four pools. Pool 1 consisted of France, Mexico, Argentina and Chile. Pool 2 had Yugoslavia, Brazil and Bolivia. Pool 3 consisted of Uruguay, Romania and Peru, while the United States, Paraguay and Belgium made up Pool 4. The winners of each section went into the semi-final. The semi-final and final would be decided on a knock-out basis.

Favourites Uruguay and Argentina duly won their way into the last four where they were joined by the USA, who surprisingly beat both Belgium and Paraguay by a similar score of 3-0, and Yugoslavia, who in their opening game had scored a notable 2-1 win over the technically brilliant Brazilians.

In the semi-finals the skilful Argentinians were much too good for the Americans and duly defeated them by six goals to one. Uruguay, urged on by their fanatical supporters, slammed Yugoslavia by the same score and thus the scene was set for an explosive final. The docks at Montevideo saw daily arrivals of ships packed tight with rabid Argentinian supporters, all thirsting for a victory over their traditional rivals.

Such was the tension on the day of the final that everyone in the crowd was searched as they filed into the Centenario Stadium. Revolvers, knives and other dangerous weapons were confiscated. The police were determined to crack down on any violence that might mar the auspicious occasion.

The Uruguayans were confident of victory. For months before the World Cup they had prepared in a secluded training camp under a no-nonsense regime. The discipline was so strict that not even their star goalkeeper, Mazzali, was exempt from breaking the night curfew; when he was discovered sneaking in late one night, he was sent home in disgrace!

A dispute arose even before the game began. The referee

came out into the blazing July sunshine carrying two footballs – one Uruguayan and the other Argentinian. Each team refused to play with the other country's football. An argument developed on the centre-spot between excited officials from both teams before it was finally decided to toss for choice. The game began amid a frenzy of excitement with the Argentinan ball being kicked off.

Fortunately for the good name of soccer, and the future of the World Cup, the game was a relatively quiet affair despite the explosive build-up. Tackling was hard but by no means vicious and the referee kept tight control. Right-winger Dorado set the stadium alight when he put the Uruguayans ahead after only 12 minutes. But Argentina refused to panic and goals by Peucelle and their new centre-forward Stabile left them leading by two goals to one at half-time.

Ten minutes after the break, inside-left Pedro Cea set all Uruguay cheering when he equalised. In the sixty-fifth minute, outside-left Santos Iriarte became a national hero when he put Uruguay ahead. Argentina fought back valiantly, but to no avail. In the closing seconds, centre-forward Castro scored again, to leave Uruguay the winners by four goals to two. Amid wild scenes, Jules Rimet proudly presented his trophy to Nasazzi, the jubilant Uruguayan captain.

Bitterly disappointed at their team's defeat, enraged supporters and officials of the Argentinian team sent up a cry of 'Robbery!' They accused the Uruguayans of breaking almost every rule in the book, and the referee of turning a blind eye to it all. Argentinian newspapers added fuel to the fire with inflammatory reports, and passions ran so high that the Uruguayan Consulate in Buenos Aires was besieged by an angry mob who fought pitched battles with the local police.

The Football Associations of the two countries broke off

relations and it was a long time before normal communications were resumed.

While all this was going on, celebrations were continuing the length and breadth of Uruguay. Fans held carnivals in the streets and the team members who played in the final were fêted and honoured like heroes.

Despite the riots and the war of words, which lasted long after the final in Montevideo, one thing was obvious to all soccer nations – as a showcase, the World Cup was here to stay.

Final

Uruguay 4	**Argentina 2**
Dorado	Peucelle
Cea	Stabile
Iriarte	
Castro	

Half-time 1-2

· URUGUAY ·

FROM the opening game of the World Cup, the brand of soccer displayed by teams battling for the coveted trophy has been of the explosive variety. Down through the years, games between national teams sporting the best players in the world have thrilled stadia packed with screeching soccer fans. The majority of the matches are played in the best sporting tradition. But occasionally something happens that will spark off a riot among the fans.

Rivalry is so intense during the World Cup that only the best referees from many different countries are selected to keep the peace during games. It seems odd, therefore, to recall that when the 1930 World Cup match between France and Argentina erupted into total disorder, the spark that ignited the powder-keg should have been set off by the referee himself.

The game was part of the preliminary round in which either Argentina or France was favoured to top their group and advance to the semi-final of the tournament proper. The French were anxious to make their mark in this distinguished tournament which their compatriot Jules Rimet had worked so hard for almost two decades to launch. They were one of only four European teams to travel to South America for this, the inaugural tournament, and they travelled with high expectations that they could win the gold trophy which bore the name of their mentor.

The French team was given the honour of starting off the tournament which they did with a Pool 1 game against Mexico on a Sunday afternoon of mid-July. Their pool also comprised the tough, talented Argentinians, who had been seeded to win the group which also included little-fancied Chile.

France swept the Mexicans aside by a four goals to one margin. Two days later they faced Argentina. The general opinion was that whichever team won this tie would top the group and advance to the semi-final. The French forwards feared Julio Monti, the no-nonsense Argentinian centre-half, a rough, tough tackler who took no prisoners.

The game itself started quietly enough and the early play gave no indication of the chaos that was to follow.

Argentina, one of the favourites for the competition, were playing like champions and launched attack after attack on the French goal. Only some excellent saves by the French goalkeeper, Thepot,14

prevented a goal, and half-time arrived with no goals scored.

The score sheet was still blank with nine minutes to go and when Argentina got a free kick just outside the French penalty area, the big man Monti stepped up to take it. He struck the ball beautifully and it flashed into the French net. With the score at one goal to nil, the South Americans fell back into defence, confident that they could prevent the French from equalising.

It was a mistake. The French suddenly found themselves with more room in which to work the ball around and their quicksilver forwards began to worry the Argentinian defence. There were still six minutes of play remaining when tricky French left-winger Marcel Langiller got the ball and bore down on the opposing goal. Beating man after man in an amazing dribble, he steadied himself and was just about to shoot for goal when Brazilian referee

Almeida Rego blew his whistle for full-time.

The crowd in the stadium were stunned. According to their watches, the official had made a terrible mistake – there were still more than five minutes of play remaining!

Thinking the game was over, the Argentinians hugged each other and, weeping tears of joy, trooped off the field and into their dressing-room to celebrate their victory. The team and their ecstatic officials were oblivious of the chaos that was breaking out above them in the stadium.

French officials and team members, assisted by thousands of howling spectators who had climbed over the wire fence on to the field, surrounded referee Rego and his two linesmen and, after much shouting and gesticulating, finally convinced the harassed official that he had made a mistake. There was only one thing he could do – order the Argentinians back onto the field and get them to face the French for five more minutes of play.

Mounted police with arms at the ready were summoned and began chasing the angry fans back over the wire fence.

Finally, the pitch was cleared and the Argentinians were enticed back. It was obvious by their angry glances to the referee that they were not too happy with the situation, but there was nothing they could do about it.

The excitement was so intense that the Argentinian inside-left and captain, Ferreira, fainted and was promptly carried off to receive attention. When the last spectator had scrambled back into the stand, the game got under way again.

With the police on the alert for any trouble, the 'lost' five minutes were played out. By this time both teams were feeling the strain of the extraordinary chain of events and, try as they might, the French could not breach the Argentinian defence. When the referee blew his whistle for full-time, the French knew their chance of winning the coveted Jules Rimet trophy was gone. But at least they had the satisfaction of knowing that they had taken part in one of the most extraordinary soccer games ever.

And what of *Senhor* Rego, the referee who had made the blunder? His handling of the explosive situation so impressed FIFA, the ruling body, that they appointed the Brazilian official to take charge of one of the vital semi-finals. Diplomacy, however, prevailed. The game was not the one in which the Argentinian team was involved!

· ITALY ·

IN 1934, the World Cup was held in Europe for the first time. Eager to stage the soccer festival that had gripped the imagination of the soccer public since its inception four years before, countries from many parts of Europe sent delegates to the 1932 Congress of the Federation of International Football Associations in Stockholm, all of them anxious to be given the honour of staging the competition.

Surprisingly, Italy, then in the grip of Mussolini's Fascist regime, was delegated to be the first European country to host the World Cup. Thirty-two nations entered, a big increase on the thirteen of 1930, so a qualifying tournament had to be arranged. Sixteen teams eventually made it to Italy and the final proper. Unlike in Uruguay, where it had been planned to play all the games in one stadium, the 1934 preliminary games were staged in several Italian cities. Another change was that the tournament in Italy was on a straightforward knock-out basis, as opposed to the group system of 1930.

Sadly, Uruguay, the holders of the Jules Rimet trophy, did not travel to Italy to defend their title as world champions. They were still feeling slighted that only four European teams had come to their country when they had hosted the tournament four years previously.

Benito Mussolini, *Il Duce*, was so anxious to claim the World Cup for his country that the Italian delegation which had gone to the FIFA congress in Stockholm two years earlier was ordered to sing the praises of Italian soccer and the facilities it could offer in various stadia, especially the excellent football grounds in Rome, Naples, Florence and Turin. The ploy worked and Mussolini got the prize he wanted.

Once again, teams from Britain and Ireland were notable absentees. England had been in dispute with FIFA since before 1930 and was not a member of the world body. Brazil and Argentina made the 8,000 mile journey from South America, the latter country weakened by the fact that Italy had claimed three of their star players through doubtful nationality claims. The United States also reached the final sixteen, defeating Mexico to gain the last place.

From the start Benito Mussolini and his followers saw the World Cup as a vehicle for promoting Fascism. *Il Duce* made it clear that he wanted a rigorous training schedule for Italy's best footballers to be organised and that Vittorio Pozzo, a man with a keen soccer brain and a martinet to boot, be put in charge. Like Hitler at the Berlin Olympics two years hence, Mussolini would dominate the tournament – and he expected to be in Rome for the final to see the Italian team take the Jules Rimet trophy.

FIFA officials obligingly turned a blind eye to the fact that the Italian team contained three Argentinian-born players, including the fearful centre-half Monti, who four years earlier had played in the World Cup final for his native country. Soccer fervour bordering on fanaticism swept Italy, and the presence of Fascists at games was a naked threat to players and referees alike. Supporters waving banners and flags made their presence known at every game in which the home side played, and opposing players and match officials came in for abuse. The message was clear – the result had to be an Italian victory, whatever the cost.

In the first round Mussolini saw his team easily defeat the United States by seven goals to one in Rome. The next game against the talented Spaniards in Florence was one that must have given the beaming dictator nightmares!

Spain took the lead with a rather fortunate goal in the first half when Regueiro half hit a shot that wrong-footed the Italian goalkeeper, Combi. The Spaniards had been shipping some heavy tackles, many of which went unpenalised, from their opponents. Centre-half Monti, especially, was throwing his weight around, a special target being Zamora, the acrobatic Spanish 'keeper, who was having an outstanding game. The Italian fans roared for an equaliser, screaming at the referee on the rare occasions he penalised one of the home players.

The second half had hardly begun when the referee gave Italy a free kick. When the ball was floated into the Spanish penalty area, the official conveniently turned a blind eye when an Italian forward seemed to obstruct Zamora as the goalkeeper rose for the high ball. The ball fell nicely for Ferrari, who cracked it into the Spanish net. The home crowd roared its delight as the referee ignored a possible foul and awarded a goal. Despite 30 minutes of extra time, the game ended in a 1-1 draw. The teams would replay the following day.

Unfortunately, the Spaniards had taken such a hammering from the Italians that they had to field five reserves – including a substitute for Zamora, who was too badly bruised to take his place in goal.

In the second game the Italians again mixed brawn with skill. Encouraged by the temerity of the Swiss referee, they laid into the Spaniards and, although the Italians scored only one goal, it was enough to see them through to the semi-final against Austria. When the final whistle blew in Italy's game against Spain, *Il Duce* smiled broadly and waved to the crowd. Meanwhile, Swiss officials, outraged at how badly their referee had handled the match, held a meeting and later suspended the official.

The Italians were victorious in the semi-final. The match was played in Milan and, although the Austrians stood up manfully to Italy and their fanatical followers, the only goal of the game was scored in the eighteenth minute by right-winger Guaita, one of the Argentinian players who had declared for Italy. Mussolini's smile grew wider as he contemplated the glory awaiting him and his followers in the final in Rome. Only the footballers of Czechoslovakia stood between Italy and the Jules Rimet trophy.

Il Duce turned out in all his splendor for the final, prepared to cheer his team on to a glorious victory. But the men from Czechoslovakia were not intimidated by the huge wave of support that was engulfing Italy. They were confident they could upset the odds and win the World Cup.

From the outset the Czechs played the neat, short-passing game which had served them well in the tournament and which looked to be paying off against the Italians. They had beaten the fancied Germany by three goals to one in the semi-final and were looking to inside-left Nejedly, who had scored two goals in that game, to do the same again. By a coincidence, both goalkeepers, Combi for Italy and Planicka for Czechoslovakia, were captains of their respective teams.

Combi was partly to blame for the Czech goal, which opened the scoring midway through the second half of a fiercely fought game. Outside-right Puc struck a speculative long shot to Combi's right, the goalkeeper inexplicably hesitated in going down on the ball – and Italy were a goal down! Up in the specially decorated enclosure in the stand, Mussolini could see his Fascist dream disintegrating before his eyes.

Italy were all at sea and Czechoslovakia had a great chance to make the game safe when a shot from inside-right Svoboda hit the upright with Combi beaten. The ball rebounded to Svoboda's team-mate Sobotka, but he inexplicably missed an open goal. Italy were looking dispirited and their forwards were making no headway against a resolute Czech defence.

One man who had not given up hope was Italian coach Vittorio Pozzo. Down on the sideline he shouted encouragement to his men, urging them on to greater efforts. Then, with only eight minutes of the game remaining, and with Czechoslovakia in control, Italy unexpectedly equalised!

It was a goal born out of sheer desperation. Outside-left, Orsi, the third Argentinian on the Italian side, got the ball 20 yards from the Czech goal. He seemed to be in two minds about what to do with it, then decided to lash it with his left foot towards Planicka in the Czech goal.

The ball swerved in mid-air, curling all the time, and dipped under the crossbar just out of reach of the bewildered goalkeeper. There was a split second of stunned silence, then the frenzied Italian fans went wild.

Thirty minutes of extra time followed. Both teams were physically drained, but urged on by their vociferous following, the Italians and the trio of Argentinians found that something extra. Pozzo was screaming instructions from the touchline and seven minutes after the restart he danced with joy when his centre-forward, Schiavio, on tired legs, rounded a Czech defender and shot past the hapless Planicka. It was still 2-1 to Italy when a relieved referee blew the final whistle. Italy had won the World Cup and Vittorio Pozzo and his players were suitably rewarded by a beaming Mussolini.

But some of the gilt was taken off the victory the following day when Orsi, fêted by the Italians as the man who had scored that amazing goal, went back to the stadium and, decked out in football gear and in front of a squad of photographers, offered to show them how he had put the ball in the net.

With no goalkeeper between the posts, he tried time and time again to curl the ball into the goal. A red-faced Orsi never came near to repeating his lucky shot of the previous day!

Final

Italy 2	**Czechoslovakia 1**
Orsi	Puc
Schiavio	

(after extra-time)

Half-time 0-0 Full-time 1-1

· FRANCE ·

THE thousands of spectators streaming into the new football stadium in Bordeaux jostled each other in their efforts to get a good vantage point from which to see the quarter-final replay between Czechoslovakia and Brazil.

A huge crowd had come in anticipation of witnessing a bruising battle similar to the one that had taken place a couple of days earlier between the two teams. In that encounter the Brazilians had eschewed their usual game, geared to total football allied with individual brilliance, to take on the solid, tough-tackling Czechs. The outcome was referred to later in local newspapers as the Battle of Bordeaux.

That first encounter had resulted in a game of bad temper and fierce tackles. Two Brazilians and a Czech player had been ordered off for rough play, two more players had finished in hospital – one with a broken leg – and two more had to be assisted from the field at the finish. By that time both teams were down to nine men and the score was 1-1.

A lot of the tension was a result of the pressure which the Brazilian team was under to return home as World Cup champions. Cuba apart, Brazil was the only team to travel to France from South America in 1938; Uruguay had stayed at home, still smarting at the refusal of many European teams to travel when they had staged the inaugural World Cup eight years earlier. Argentina, angry at not being allowed to stage the tournament, had also declined to travel to France.

With their potential Cup-winning South American neighbours eliminating themselves, the Brazilians felt confident of bringing home the Jules Rimet trophy. The team left for the long journey to Europe with the backing of their government and a rousing send-off from the fans.

The tournament was decided on a straightforward knock-out basis and Brazil lived dangerously in their first match against Poland in Strasbourg. The game went to extra time and eleven goals were scored, with Brazil coming out on top by six goals to five. Amazingly, two men scored four goals each in that game – Brazil's centre-forward Leonidas and the blond inside-left Willimowski for Poland.

It was the South Americans' next game, however, that really provided the fireworks. The iron men of Czechoslovakia held no fear of the Brazilians. They had narrowly lost to Italy in the World Cup final four years before, and their 1938 team included several survivors from that time. These included mercurial inside-left Nejedly, a masterly ball player whose penchant was scoring goals from half chances. He was a marked man from the outset; the Brazilians knew he had to be stopped at all costs.

The game had barely started when Brazil's right-half, the robust Zeze, ignored the ball completely and kicked Nejedly instead. The Hungarian referee had no hesitation in sending Zeze to the sideline.

Despite being reduced to ten men, the Brazilians surged forward and Leonidas, nicknamed the Black Diamond, gave them the lead after half-an-hour. Brazil were reduced to nine men just before half-time when Riha, the Czech outside-right, and his marker Machados came to blows. Both were ordered off by the referee.

Even though they were playing with only nine men against the ten Czechoslovakians, the Brazilians held on to their slender 1-0 lead until fifteen minutes into the second half when full-back Da Guia, in a moment of madness, handled the ball. Despite the rough treatment he had received during the game, Nejedly was able to equalise from the penalty spot.

The score remained 1-1 until the final whistle. Extra-time brought its quota of dreadful fouls, but no further goals. Brazil had the audacity to claim that the Czechoslovakians were responsible for the Battle of Bordeaux, and that the game should be awarded to them. Their pleas were rightly dismissed by the tournament governing body.

Fans packed the stadium a few days later for the replay, expecting to see another bruising battle. The Czechs had taken such a hammering in the first encounter that they had to field six reserves. Their first choice goalkeeper Planicka had sustained a broken arm in the earlier game and a reserve took his place. Also missing from the Czech line-up was Nejedly. He had not recovered from his injuries, and his omission was seen as a grievous loss to the team.

Brazil also made changes – nine in all. Some were necessary because of injuries, but so confident were the team selectors of victory in the replay that most of their best players were rested in anticipation of the next round game against Italy in Marseille. It was an audacious gamble.

Just before the two teams took the field, the Brazilians received a telegram from prominent people back home wishing them success. The wire itself contained only six words, but below the text was a long list of names pledging undying support for the players.

Earlier, Brazilian goalkeeper Walter had been promised a

huge sum of money by another wealthy supporter if he kept the Czechs from scoring. When this story broke in the newspapers, it added to the tension as kick-off time neared.

The fans who had come to the replay expecting another war were disappointed. This time, both teams concentrated on playing football and the game passed off with no ugly fouls. A change of referee – the Hungarian official had been replaced by a Frenchman – also helped calm the atmosphere. A large force of gendarmes patrolled the ground in case of trouble.

Early in the first half, goalkeeper Walter saw a small fortune slip away from him when Kopecky, the man who had replaced the injured Nejedly, shot the ball past him into the net.

But this time the Brazilians did not resort to tough tactics. They kept their composure, playing the type of football expected of them, and they scored twice in the second half through Leonidas and Roberto, to run out worthy winners.

Then it was on to Marseille and the semi-final against Italy, holders of the trophy. Back in Brazil, excitement was intense in expectation of the team making it to the final and returning home with the Cup. Earlier, a telegram had arrived at the squad's headquarters from the president of the Brazilian Football Federation promising the players that if they succeeded in winning the trophy, they each would receive a house in token of the nation's appreciation. But first, Italy had to be defeated in the semi-final.

Amazingly, the arrogant Brazilians rested Leonidas, easily their best forward, for this important game. They wanted him to be at his best for the final after they had defeated the Italians. It was a ploy that did not go down well with some players in the team.

The game turned into a nightmare for the elegant Brazilian full-back Domingas Da Guia, the man who had given away a needless penalty against Czechoslovakia. Several times in the first half the big, bustling Italian centre-forward Piola, went past Da Guia, making him look very ordinary indeed. When Piola did the same thing in the fourteenth minute, the frustrated Da Guia whipped the Italian's legs out from under him in the penalty area. Meazza, Italy's captain, crashed home the spot kick and his team were two goals up, winger Colaussi having netted earlier.

Brazil improved in the second half and put the Italians under tremendous pressure. Time and time again it looked as if their skilful football would breach the Italian defence, but they had 'rested' their great goal-getter, Leonidas, and he was badly missed. Two of Brazil's best chances fell to Peracio, the man deputising for Leonidas, but he was not as deadly around the goal area as the Black Diamond, and both chances were missed.

Only three minutes of the game remained when inside-left, Romeo, pulled one back for Brazil. Spurred on by the riches awaiting them back home if they won the Jules Rimet trophy, the South Americans tried desperately for the equaliser as the seconds ticked away. Three minutes later the referee blew the final whistle. Italy had triumphed by 2-1 and the Brazilian dream was shattered once again.

In Brazil, the result was greeted with incredulity and not a little anger from the soccer-mad populace. The team selectors came under fire for their arrogance and bad judgement in resting their best players in crucial games. Fuel was added to the fire a few days later when, in the play-off for third place against Sweden, the other losing semi-finalists, the Brazilians won 4-2, with favourite son Leonidas scoring two excellent goals.

Meanwhile, Italy had gone on to defeat Hungary by four goals to two in the final to retain the title they had won four years previously.

The Brazilians made the long journey home and were greeted as failures. The 'houses for all' promise had evaporated and, worse still, with a war looming in Europe, it would be twelve years before the footballers from Brazil would get another opportunity to win the coveted trophy. Next time around they would have no excuses for failure – the 1950 World Cup would be held in their own country.

Final

Italy 4	**Hungary 2**
Colaussi (2)	Titkos
Piola (2)	Sarosi

Half-time 3-1

· BRAZIL (1) ·

WHEN England made their debut in the World Cup in 1950 they travelled to Brazil as one of the favourites to win the famed trophy. And the sparse thousands of fans who bothered to travel to out-of-the-way Belo Horizonte to see the powerful English team take on the footballers of the United States, did so in anticipation of a goal feast.

The scenario was that England, the acknowledged masters of the game, would crush a US team of disparate nationalities and dubious talent. Even the several thousand partisan Brazilians, who had come in the hope of seeing one of the favourites humbled, acknowledged that it would be a miracle were it to happen.

The English soccer authorities had settled their differences with FIFA, the world ruling body, and hopes were high that the team could return home with the Jules Rimet in its possession. The English travelled to South America having appointed their first full-time manager, Walter Winterbottom. He had a squad of stars that included world-famous names like Wilf Mannion, Stanley Matthews, Tom Finney, Billy Wright, Alf Ramsey, Stan Mortensen and Jackie Milburn.

The American team, on the other hand, was composed of a hotch-potch of players, many of whom had sampled football in countries other than the US. The mixture of soccer skills was exemplified by names like Souza, Colombo, McIlvenny and goalkeeper Borghi. Indeed before coming to live in America Eddie McIlvenny had been let go by an English Third-Division club! Canny Scots coach Bill Jeffrey had welded together his League of Nations team and hoped they would give a good account of themselves in the tournament.

In the earlier Group 2 games, England, playing in the giant Maracana stadium in Rio de Janeiro, had struggled in the heat to defeat Chile by two goals to nil. In the other group game Spain were also unimpressive in overcoming the US. Only by scoring three goals in the final ten minutes did Spain escape an embarrassing defeat.

England were joint favourites with the brilliant Brazilians to win the trophy and become world champions, while the US were quoted at 500-1 outsiders... and some even thought those odds generous! The game was reckoned such a foregone conclusion that it was played in unfashionable Belo Horizonte where the pitch was small and bumpy and facilities barely adequate. So confident was England team selector Arthur Drewry of victory that he rested several of his top stars for the anticipated sterner tests which lay ahead.

When the two teams lined up before kick-off, the difference between them was almost laughable. The English players looked superbly fit, they were immaculately togged out and eager for action. By contrast, the US side looked exactly what they were – a bunch of footballers brought together from different backgrounds, hoping to keep the score down to respectable proportions. Several of the players wore odd stockings and they rated their chances against the English masters so low that some of them had broken the night curfew and had stayed up until the early hours drinking in a local hostelry.

When the game got under way, it looked as if it was going to be a slaughter of the innocents. Roared on by a couple of thousand English workers from a nearby goldmine, the English swept forward in search of a hatful of goals. Only a couple of miracle saves by Borghi kept the ball out of the US net. When he was finally beaten, Milburn's shot hit the post and came back into play.

At right-half for the US side, captain Eddie McIlvenny, the man who could not make the grade in England, was having a storming game. Time and time again he broke up English attacks and his intelligent passing to his forwards, including the elusive John Souza, was troubling the English defence.

When half an hour had passed without the vaunted English forward line scoring, their supporters began to get restless. The bumpy pitch was not suited to England's flowing style of play and passes were going astray. A touch of desperation had crept into the English players' game, while the US team began to grow in confidence.

Then the incredible happened: the US scored! Eight minutes before half-time England were on the attack when once again McIlvenny intercepted and a swift pass set his own forwards moving. Flaxen-haired Bert Williams in the English goal had not had a worthwhile shot to deal with all afternoon and moved forward confidently to avert the danger.

It was not clear whether the American player, left-half Bahr, had meant to cross the ball or shoot at goal. Williams came out to gather the ball in mid-air, but before he could do so, it glanced off the head of Haitian-born centre forward Gaetjens and finished in the English net.

For a split second the crowd was silent. Then a roar went up that must have been heard in Rio! It was a goal that rocked the soccer world and was destined to be talked about for years.

From the kick-off England went on the attack again and they stayed in the US half until the whistle blew for half-time. Still, England had not found the net.

Could the underdogs hold out until the final whistle? Roared on by the excited locals who anticipated a sensation in the making, the American team played like men inspired. Coach Walter Winterbottom made changes in the English forward line, but try as they might, great players like Mortensen, Finney and Mannion could not get the ball past Borghi in the US goal. Towards the end, English full-back Ramsey floated a free kick into the opposing penalty area. It was headed towards goal by inside-forward Chris Mullen, but just before it could cross the line an American boot kicked it clear.

That was England's last chance. Minutes later the final whistle blew and it was all over. The tournament joint-favourites had been beaten by the 500-1 outsiders. Brazilian fans lit newspapers in the stands in celebration while hundreds of spectators invaded the pitch and carried the jubilant US players off shoulder high. The look of disbelief on the faces of the English squad as they trooped dejectedly off to the dressing-room said it all.

When the word got back to Rio de Janeiro that England had been defeated in Belo Horizonte there were many who did not, at first, believe the result. In America, the *New York Times*, convinced that the story coming in over the wires was a hoax, refused to print the result until it had been confirmed by their official correspondent.

Meanwhile, the American team manager was frantically switching dates on airline tickets. He had been so sure that his team would be defeated, he had booked them home on an early flight! Now there was the chance they could defeat Chile and finish top of their group.

Sadly it was not to be. A few days later Chile beat the US by five goals to two and the outsiders were out of the World Cup. But the team members had had their hour of glory in Belo Horizonte and they had the satisfaction of knowing that their famous victory had been recorded in newspapers around the world.

What a pity, then, that when they returned home, they were not accorded the traditional ticker-tape welcome in New York to mark their amazing achievement.

Argentina's Guillermo Stabile (arm raised) scores his side's second goal against Uruguay in the 1930 World Cup final in Montevideo.

Hector Castro (left of right-hand upright) scores Uruguay's fourth goal in the 1930 World Cup final as an Argentinian defender tries unsuccessfully to prevent the ball entering the net. (Popperfoto)

Italian captain Combi (left) greets Czechoslovakia's Planicka before the start of the 1934 World Cup final in Rome. By a strange coincidence, both captains were goalkeepers.

The Italian team, with coach Victor Pozzo, which went on to win the 1934 World Cup in front of Il Duce Benito Mussolini. (Popperfoto)

England goalkeeper Bert Williams saves during the game against the U.S. in the 1950 World Cup. This encounter in Belo Horizonte produced an amazing result. (Popperfoto)

Sandor Hidegkuti scores Hungary's second goal in the epic semi-final against Uruguay in Lausanne during the 1954 World Cup.

Ferenc Puskas scores Hungary's first goal against West Germany in the 1954 final in Berne, as goalkeeper Turek looks on helplessly. (Popperfoto)

Vava equalises for Brazil in the game against Sweden in the 1958 World Cup final after the home side had unexpectedly scored first. (Popperfoto)

Brazilian teenager Pelé (extreme left) scores his side's third goal against Sweden in the 1958 World Cup final in Stockholm. On the terraces, the samba beat rings out in triumph. (Colorsport)

A lap of honour by Brazil after they defeated Sweden in the 1958 final. (Popperfoto)

Czechoslovakian defender Populhar clears from Pelé with a high kick in the 1962 final in Santiago, Chile. (Popperfoto)

North Korea's Pak Doo scores his side's first goal in the sensational defeat of Italy in the 1966 World Cup. (Popperfoto)

· BRAZIL (2) ·

THE sun beat down with a fierce intensity on the record crowd of 200,000 wildly cheering fans packed into the giant Maracana Stadium in Rio de Janeiro that Sunday afternoon in 1950.

For many months previously there had been only one topic of conversation in soccer-crazy Brazil: the World Cup tournament, now reaching its climax after almost three weeks of nail-biting excitement. The two teams which had emerged to do battle in the final were red-hot favourites Brazil, urged on by a fanatical home support, and their deadly rivals Uruguay, very definitely the outsiders.

Day after day the previous week, thousands of excited Brazilian soccer fans had poured into the city, many of them without tickets, but all of them determined to see their countrymen win the Jules Rimet trophy for the first time. Newspapers and radio were putting out endless reports about the forthcoming final and they had whipped up the fervour of the fans to fever pitch.

Adding to the chaos was the fact that the Maracana Stadium, which the authorities had ordered to be built specially to house the World Cup games, was still unfinished when the tournament began. Even on final day, mounds of rubble were still lying around outside, over which the excited Brazilian fans scrambled to gain entrance.

Inside the stadium, however, everything was perfection with nothing left to chance. A six-foot moat had been dug around the pitch just in case things got out of hand.

Policemen, armed to the teeth, and with orders to use whatever means possible to maintain order, patrolled the ground. The Brazilian fans were in a happy mood; their team was an overwhelming favourite to defeat the Uruguayans.

Incredibly only 13 teams had entered the 1950 World Cup, the same number as had entered 20 years previously in Uruguay when the tournament was first held. In Brazil, the 13 teams had been split into four groups. Pools 1 and 2 had four teams, Pool 3 had three teams, with Pool 4 containing only two. The four winners of each group would then form a final pool; they would play each other, with the team with the most number of points claiming the trophy as world champions.

Brazil had topped the tough Pool 1 where they had beaten Mexico and Yugoslavia and drawn with Switzerland. Uruguay was in the farcical Pool 4 where they had only to overwhelm a weak Bolivian team 8-0 to join Spain, Sweden and Brazil in the final group.

In their first two games in the final pool the rampant Brazilians crushed Sweden 7-1 and then ran rings around a useful Spanish side, winning by 6-1. Uruguay, on the other hand, could only draw 2-2 with Spain and had struggled to beat Sweden by the odd goal in five. Thus, Brazil had only to draw their final game with Uruguay in the Maracana Stadium and they would become world champions. No wonder their fans filled the giant stadium! Although Uruguay had already beaten Brazil earlier that year, such was the euphoria among the home fans that the only question to be answered was by how many goals their team would win. With the dynamic inside forward trio of Zizinho, Ademar and Jair the confident Brazilian fans felt that goals were sure to flow.

The fans were not the only ones to be lulled into a false sense of victory. Before the game started, the Governor of Rio hailed his countrymen as world champions and told them: 'You have no equals in the terrestrial hemisphere'. Team manager Flavio Costa was not quite so sure; he warned his players not to walk out onto the pitch before the game feeling that the world championship was already theirs.

If the Brazilian team bristled with big names, the men from Uruguay were little behind in talent, and certainly did not lack in commitment. In centre-half they had Obdulio Varela, a giant of a player in stature and in spirit. Goalkeeper Maspoli was cat-like, while up front the mustachioed Alcide Ghiggia was an opportunist outside-right. Inside-left Juan Schiaffino's tall, thin frame ghosted past opponents with ease, and he was a deadly marksman in the penalty area.

When the Brazilian players emerged from the tunnel onto the pitch, they were greeted with a noisy fireworks display. By contrast, when the Uruguayans appeared there was hardly a cheer. The capacity crowd filled the three-tiered Maracana Stadium to bursting point and they fell silent only for the respective national anthems. As soon as the referee blew his whistle to start the game, the Brazilian crowd began screaming encouragement.

Their team responded by going on an all-out attack and laying siege on the Uruguayan goal. Varela and his team-mates strove desperately to deal with the quicksilver passing and the darting runs of Zizinho, Ademar and Jair. Time and time again only a last-second tackle by a Uruguayan defender prevented disaster. In goal, Maspoli was performing near miracles.

Halfway through the first half, Brazil looked certain to score when Jair let fly a rocket of a shot. Somehow the black-clad Maspoli got a hand to it and deflected it for a corner. Brazil forced several more corners, all of which were cleared. Ademar threw his hands up in frustration when, alone in front of goal, he shot powerfully, only for Maspoli to fling himself sideways and save. The crowd groaned. At the other end Brazilian 'keeper Barbosa was virtually a spectator.

Ten minutes before half-time Barbosa had to leap into sudden action to save a shot from Schiaffino after the Uruguayans had, at last, raised the siege and mounted a swift attack. But soon Brazil were back on the offensive and Jair was unlucky when his shot beat Maspoli but hit a post. Unbelievably, half-time arrived with the score still 0-0.

During the interval, arguments raged among the huge crowd. Surely Maspoli in the Uruguayan goal could not survive another 45 minutes without being beaten? Was another huge surprise on the cards? The fans remembered an earlier game in the competition when no-hopers America had humbled mighty England 1-0 in Belo Horizonte....

The game had barely restarted when the fears of the home crowd were put at rest. Brazil scored! Ademar and Zizinho performed a bit of magic between them, a swift pass unhinged the Uruguayan defence, and outside-right Friaca stormed in to power the ball past Maspoli. At last! A roar of relief erupted from thousands of throats.

Fireworks exploded and tons of streamers were unleashed. The fans sat back to await the goal feast.

It did not materialise. The Uruguayans settled themselves and sent tremors of anxiety among the hostile Brazilian crowd by coming out of their shell and setting up some dangerous attacks. Such was the excitement that a fan collapsed and his body was taken away on a stretcher. It was a dark omen for what was to follow.

As the underdogs pressed forward, powered by the surging runs of Varela and with the elegant Schiaffino now beginning to spray passes about, it was noticeable that the Brazilians were losing their rhythm. No longer were they looking confident. Before the game their manager had warned of overconfidence; now Flavio Costa was off the bench and looking anxious.

After twenty minutes the towering figure of Varela came forward into the Brazilian half on a surging run. His pass sent Ghiggia away down the right wing. Ghiggia's precise centre found Schiaffino lurking in the penalty area. His shot gave Barbosa no chance and Uruguay were level. The crowd was stunned.

Now the Brazilian fans were on their feet, screaming at their team to pull themselves together and get back into the game. But fear of defeat was corroding confidence and disrupting the once smooth flow of passes. Not even the monastic three months of training which the Brazilian players had undergone at a villa outside Rio before the tournament could save them. Was the unthinkable about to happen?

With eleven minutes of the game left, a series of passes between Perez and Ghiggia saw the latter free of his marker and bearing down on Barbosa in the Brazilian goal. Ghiggia shot – and the ball was in the net once again. Uruguay were ahead 2-1.

As the precious minutes ticked away, the Brazilians, urged on by the now frantic crowd, threw caution to the winds and mounted attack after attack. Defenders moved forward and in the last despairing minutes even full-back and captain Augusto came up into the Uruguayan penalty area in an effort to score the vital equaliser. The once brilliant Brazilian forwards were now easy meat for the quick-tackling Uruguayan defenders.

The final whistle shrilled with the Brazilians still trying to score the goal that would bring the game into extra-time. It did not happen and at the end it was Obdulio Varela who walked up the steps ahead of his triumphant team-mates to receive the

Jules Rimet trophy. He had played a captain's part in the victory and would return home a national hero.

The World Cup, after a twenty-year span and a victory against all the odds, was on its way back to Montevideo. While the celebrations went on for weeks in Uruguay, Brazil descended into the depths of what could best be described as a period of national mourning.

Later it was revealed that the excitement had been so intense during those last few minutes of the game that three fans listening to a radio broadcast of the match 1,000 miles away in Montevideo had died of heart attacks.

In Rio itself, a newspaper editor had been so confident that Brazil would win that he had printed his newspaper before the match started, with bold headlines proclaiming them world champions. He had reckoned without the fighting Uruguayans.

Final

Brazil 1	**Uruguay 2**
Friaca	Schiaffino
	Ghiggia

Half-time 0-0

· SWITZERLAND (1) ·

IT is to be expected that when sixteen of the world's top teams come to grips in the battle for the premier prize in soccer, fits of temper and ugly displays of bad sportsmanship will occasionally surface. Unfortunately, even the most talented footballers have been known to resort to doubtful tactics in the pursuit of glory.

When Hungary and Brazil were drawn against one another in the quarter-final stages of the 1954 World Cup in Switzerland, the fans looked forward to what they reckoned would be a classic encounter between two of the favourites. It was an eagerly awaited clash between teams universally recognised as the champions of Europe and South America.

As far as the fans were concerned, these were the two best teams in the tournament and this could well rate as the World Cup final itself. The stadium was packed for the game between two teams who relied on total football. Instead of the anticipated soccer classic, however, it turned out to be what one writer aptly described later as the 'Battle of Berne'.

For most of the 90 minutes these 22 football artists kicked, punched, pulled and pummelled to such a degree that three players were sent off, two penalties were awarded, and the referee had to issue four warnings.

After the game, the battle raged in the Hungarian dressing-room which was invaded by incensed Brazilian players and officials. The incidents witnessed there by members of the media were among the worst ever seen in a soccer stadium.

Yet it could have been so different had both teams concentrated on playing football instead of waging war. Hungary was reckoned to be the best team in the world at the time. They had burst on the scene in 1953, sensationally defeating England 6-3 at Wembley, playing a style of football never seen up to then. England had never before been beaten at Wembley, but they were overwhelmed by a team which contained seven players from the army club, Honved.

A few weeks before the World Cup finals in Switzerland, the Hungarians had proved that the Wembley result was no fluke by again defeating England – this time by a 7-1 margin in Budapest.

The team had players whose names have since become part of soccer folklore: Ferenc Puskas, a chubby inside-left and ball juggler whose armoury included a ferocious left-foot shot; inside-right Sandor 'Golden Head' Kocsis, whose prodigious leaps in the penalty area delighted the fans, and centre-forward Sandor Hidegkuti, an expert at bullet-like shots from long range. Wingers Budai and Czibor were speedy, incisive and dangerous. Goalkeeper Gyula Grosics was a superb athlete, while midfielder Josef Bozsik was an elegant defender who went forward at every opportunity.

The Brazilians had come to Switzerland with high hopes of winning their first-ever World Cup and were little behind the Magical Magyars in skill and firepower. They had two brilliant full-backs called Santos, the black Djalma and the skilful Nilton. Pinheiro was an inspiring captain at centre-half, while the forwards boasted Didi, master of the swerving shot, and a dangerous winger in Julinho.

The Hungarians had not tasted defeat in the previous four years and had been crowned Olympic Games champions in 1952. In their two previous games in Pool 2 in Switzerland they had scored 17 goals, beating Korea 9-0 and Germany 8-3. Even allowing for the wily Germans fielding a weak team against Puskas & Co. (they were confident of advancing to the next stage), it was still an awesome performance from the Hungarians.

In their previous games in Pool 1, Brazil had destroyed Mexico by 5-0, but had been held to a 1-1 draw by the talented Yugoslavs. The Brazilians were a team of ball jugglers whose fiery temperaments and determination to win could, on occasion, be weaknesses which would militate against them. They certainly allowed those attributes to get out of control in Berne.

It did not do much for the Brazilian team's composure when Hungary went two goals up in the first eight minutes of their encounter. Hidegkuti got the first after only three minutes, despite having his shorts pulled off in the process by a despairing Brazilian defender. The pelting rain did not seem to hamper the Magyars, who soon went two goals up through Kocsis.

Incensed, the Brazilians began to cut up rough. The Hungarians may have been skilful footballers, but they also had their quota of tough men who were not slow to retaliate. The game began to deteriorate into a series of senseless fouls and ugly incidents.

Puskas, injured in the game against Germany, sat in helpless fury on the sideline as the ill-tempered match progressed. Even he could hardly object after seventeen minutes when his full-back team-mate Buzansky lashed into Brazilian centre-forward Indio and the referee pointed to the penalty spot. Djalma Santos slammed in the spot-kick and now Brazil were only one goal behind. It was 2-1 to the Hungarians at half-time.

The second period was just as ill-tempered as the first, and the referee had his hands full trying to control the game. Hungary went 3-1 up when Pinheiro handled and Lantos scored from the penalty spot. With twenty minutes to go Brazil scored again. Now the game really got out of hand.

In the heat of the moment Nilton Santos and Bozsik forgot all about football and instead squared off and began to throw punches at each other. The referee had no hesitation in sending the two of them off. While the official's back was turned, Hungarian winger Czibor was being pursued around the field by two irate Brazilians. Fortunately he managed to dodge the punches they threw at him! At one stage the Brazilian trainer dashed onto the pitch and made for the referee. The official immediately signalled for police help. Hordes of cameramen invaded the pitch and added to the confusion.

With three minutes to go and fist-fights becoming more frequent than passes, Kocsis scored with one of his spectacular headers, making the score 4-2 to Hungary. Still the drama in the rain wasn't finished. Just before the final whistle blew, Brazilian inside-left Tozzi aimed a kick in frustration at a Hungarian player and was given his marching orders.

The players trooped off, scowling and swearing at each other, with officials from both teams joining in. A few minutes later, one of the most sordid episodes in the history of the World Cup occurred when the Brazilians stormed the Hungarian dressing-room. The Battle of Berne wasn't over yet....

More fist-fights broke out, and boots and bottles were swung during the vicious exchanges. The fracas resulted in Brazilian centre-half and captain Pinheiro leaving the stadium with a bandage covering a gaping face wound – and several other players nursing injuries to add to those they had picked up on the playing field!

Amid all the confusion, one man remained unruffled and calm. He was the referee. In the cauldron that was the World Cup, he had successfully handled one of the roughest soccer games ever played. For Englishman Mr Arthur Ellis, it was perhaps the greatest achievement of a distinguished career.

· SWITZERLAND (2) ·

IT is acknowledged that the World Cup, as a sporting spectacle, brings out the best – and sometimes the worst – in teams and individuals. National sides engage in a long, drawn-out battle to qualify for the finals, and when that stage is reached, more often than not the brand of football displayed is of the highest standard.

In the finals of the 1954 tournament, one game so enraptured the soccer critics that they almost ran out of superlatives when they came to describe it. The pundits were in accord on one thing – the Hungary versus Uruguay semi-final encounter got their unanimous vote as the best game of the tournament.

The pity was that both these superb teams should clash at the semi-final stage. From the very beginning they were by far the outstanding teams of the tournament. Both had topped their sections with something to spare: Hungary scoring 17 goals in the process in Pool 2, while in Pool 3 Uruguay, the World Cup holders, had cast aside their usual robust game and instead served up a classy brand of football, to the delight of the spectators. In topping their pool, they had not lost a game. They had annihilated Scotland by 7-0 with their slightly built inside-left Juan Schiaffino the inspiration behind some deadly forward play. Thus, Uruguay had maintained their proud record of never being beaten in a World Cup tie.

Both teams had had to survive tough games in the last eight to reach the semi-final. Uruguay had claimed England's scalp in Basle, winning 4-2, with Schiaffino outstanding and scoring a goal. Hungary had survived an ugly encounter against Brazil in the 'Battle of Berne'.

And so the stage was set for what the fans reckoned would be a classic game. The opinion was that whichever team won through to the final would almost certainly account for either West Germany or Austria, who would meet in the other semi-final.

The Hungary/Uruguay clash lived up to everything that was expected of it. The two teams served up a soccer feast that tingled with tension, went into extra-time, and in the end left the spectators in the packed stadium in Lausanne wanting more. It was a clash of the Titans – the skilful South Americans against the best team in Europe. Hungary were without the injured Puskas, a vital cog in their goal-scoring machine, but Uruguay had to field without Varela, their giant centre-half and, at 39 years of age, a veteran of the cup-winning side four years before.

The excitement was intense as the European side kicked off. Both teams threw caution to the wind and immediately set up sweeping attacks that seemed set to yield a hatful of goals. The Uruguayans looked the more skilful, with the slight figure of Schiaffino riding tackles and setting up chances for his fellow attackers Ambrois and Borges. For Hungary, Kocsis and Hidegkuti went close to scoring early on. And it was those two in the fifteenth minute who set up left-winger Czibor, who lashed the ball past Maspoli to open the scoring.

Thanks to the stalwart work of defenders on both sides, particularly goalkeepers Maspoli and Grosics, Czibor's was the only goal scored before the interval. It looked all over for Uruguay early in the second half when centre-half Carballo, deputising for Varela, gave the ball away to Hungary's Budai, who crossed for the ever-dangerous Sandor Hidegkuti to head past Maspoli into the net.

Two goals down against the Magical Magyars would have knocked the fight out of most teams. But Uruguay were no ordinary outfit. They had a proud, unbeaten World Cup record to maintain and they were not going to surrender it easily. Schiaffino was everywhere, his deft touches and flashing forays towards the Hungarian goal inspiring his colleagues. The spectators, mainly Europeans, sportingly got behind the Uruguayans and urged them on to greater efforts. They responded by laying siege to the Hungarian goal with Schiaffino and centre-forward Juan Hohberg going close.

The stadium erupted when, with only fifteen minutes to go in this pulsating tie, Uruguay at last scored. Schiaffino supplied the pass for Hohberg to volley past Grosics to make it 2-1 for the Hungarians. But time was ticking away.

The crowd kept up a continuous roar as play swept from end to end at a blistering pace. Then with just three minutes of normal time remaining, and excitement at fever pitch, the Uruguayans equalised. Juan Schiaffino again performed a bit of football magic, a pass to Hohberg, and the latter volleyed the ball past Grosics.

Poor Hohberg – his team-mates were so overjoyed that he passed out under their over-zealous congratulations and he played the rest of the game in a daze!

The Hungarians were stunned by the turn of events and had to hang on grimly before the referee blew for the end of normal time. The short break before extra-time began gave them a chance to recover. Captain and right-half Bozsik used his influence to calm his colleagues. He told them he was confident they could see off their opponents during the extra 30 minutes of play.

A short distance away the Uruguayans were listening to their coach. They were bubbling over with confidence, anxious for the match to restart. The referee called both teams back and the game was on.

Once again the teams threw caution to the wind and went on an all-out attack. Within two minutes Schiaffino again split the Hungarian defence and put Hohberg through. But the centre-forward, still not fully recovered from the treatment of his colleagues, did not hit the ball properly and his shot hit the post. That was the best opportunity for a goal in the opening period. Two weary teams faced each other for the final fifteen minutes, still on level terms.

The Uruguayans were to regret that miss by Juan Hohberg. In the second period of extra-time, the tireless midfielder Andrade was injured in a tackle and had to go off for treatment. It was while his team were down to ten men that Hungarian outside-right Budai centred the ball and the deadly Kocsis rose majestically to head it past Maspoli.

The South Americans refused to throw in the towel and surged forward again in search of the equaliser. In their eagerness to attack, they left gaps at the back, and seven minutes from time their fate was sealed when Kocsis headed another excellent goal. Time ticked away and all too soon the best match of the 1956 World Cup was over, with the Hungarians winning 4-2.

As the two teams trooped wearily off the field, the crowd rose as one and showed their appreciation in round after round of applause. The masters of Europe had defeated the wizards of Latin America, and the 120 minutes of scintillating football had produced six splendid goals worthy of the World Cup. At the after-match press conference, Hungarian coach Gyula Mandi told reporters that Uruguay were the best team his men had ever come up against.

In the other semi-final, underdogs West Germany had overwhelmed a hotly fancied Austria by 6-1 before 58,000 spectators in Berne. It was an astonishing result to a game which the elegant Austrians were expected to win against a German side which was solid but unspectacular. The West Germans would be no push-overs against Hungary in the final.

In the earlier rounds of the tournament, the Germans and Hungarians had clashed in Pool 2. On that occasion the rampant Hungarians had won 8-3. But wily German coach Sepp Herberger, confident his side would later qualify, had fielded several second-choice players. They would be at full strength in the final.

There was a distinct warning for the Hungarians when their former opponents, Uruguay, met Austria to decide third and fourth places a few days later. Still not recovered from the titanic semi-final encounter, the Latins were pale shadows of their former selves and were beaten 3-1. Thus the team of many talents returned home with scant reward for their endeavours.

Would the same fate befall the Hungarians against the Germans when they met in the World Cup final the following day? Hungarian coach Gyula Mandi was a worried man. His star forward Ferenc Puskas was still not fully recovered from injury, but was insisting he should be selected. The Magical Magyars were clear favourites to beat the Germans. Could they rise once more to the occasion and be crowned world champions? The answer to that question would come in a final that provided sensations both on and off the pitch.

· SWITZERLAND (3) ·

WHEN Hungary and West Germany met in the final of the World Cup before a packed stadium in Berne, it was an unusual occasion in that it was the second time in which the two teams had clashed in the tournament.

In the early encounter, when they were both drawn in Pool 2, the multi-talented Hungarians had overwhelmed the unspectacular West Germans by 8-3. An incident in that game, however, was to play a significant part when the two teams clashed in the final a couple of weeks later.

That incident occurred half-an-hour into the game when the big, blond West German centre-half Werner Liebrich caught Hungarian inside-left Ferenc Puskas in a crunching tackle which left Puskas clutching his ankle in pain and hobbling badly. Puskas was unable to continue and left the field in pain. Later, he was to say that nothing would convince him that Liebrich's tackle and the injury to the ankle were not deliberate.

Puskas was unable to take his place in the Hungarian squad in the next two games, against Brazil in the quarter-final and Uruguay in the semi-final. He was still far from fully fit when the final against old opponents West Germany loomed, but it was known that he was arguing with team coach Gyula Mandi and insisting on being selected for the game to decide who would win the World Cup. Some team-mates reckoned that even a half-fit Puskas should be selected for the big game; others were not so sure.

Puskas was not only an inspirational captain and consistent goal-scorer for Hungary; he was a mega star in a team that bristled with talent. The team combined hitherto unseen skills on the ball with deadly shooting within the 30-yard range. In any one game it was reckoned that 80 per cent of Hungarian shots at goal hit the target.

An officer in the Hungarian army, nicknamed Puskas, 'The Galloping Major', was the target for all defenders. Mark him out of the game and the Magyars were vulnerable. He had already shown his goal-scoring skills in a 9-0 defeat of South Korea in Zurich with two goals, and for half-an-hour in the first game against Germany he was magnificent. Then came that terrible tackle by Liebrich.

From that game on, the methodical, muscular Germans showed improved form in every encounter. The all-round fitness and seemingly boundless energy displayed by the team, captained by veteran Fritz Walter, amazed onlookers and was a source of much comment in the media.

As game succeeded game, 'Fritzie' played more like a frisky schoolboy than a 33-year-old in the autumn of his career. All the Germans seemed to have unlimited energy, even at the end of a hard match. This phenomenon was to be a source of a drug charge sensation by the Hungarians after the the teams met in the final.

In the semi-final, the West Germans had annihilated an Austrian team that had crushed Czechoslovakia 5-0 and then eliminated hosts Switzerland by seven goals to five in an epic encounter. It was reckoned that the Austrians would carry too much class for the hard-working Germans.

Once again the form book was turned upside down. The West Germans, in front of a capacity 58,000 in Basle, played like men inspired. No longer were they a one-dimensional team, grinding opponents into the ground with precise but predictable play. Now they were full of fire, their sweeping attacks hitting the Austrian defence in wave after wave. The Austrian coach had made the mistake of bringing back experienced but out-of-form goalkeeper Walter Zeman and the Germans gave him a torrid time. On six occasions Zeman had to pick the ball out of his net, with the Walter brothers, Fritz and Otmar, claiming two each. It was a sensational result.

In the days before the final, frantic efforts were made in the Hungarian camp to get Puskas fully fit. Indeed, the Germans sportingly offered help to this end but it was refused. Was this another psychological ploy by Sepp Herberger or was it genuine? The Galloping Major insisted on taking his place in the line-up for the final. Puskas apart, practically every other Hungarian player needed medical treatment for injuries sustained in the games against Brazil and Uruguay.

The big game began with rain pelting down, and with the pitch becoming heavy it was obvious that stamina would play an important part in the outcome. Within six minutes Puskas silenced his critics when he blasted a left-foot shot past Turek in the German goal after the ball had been deflected to him off a defender. Two minutes later Turek fumbled a back pass and outside-right Czibor pounced and drove the ball home. 2-0 to Hungary. The final was going according to form.

Undeterred, the Germans stormed back and made it 2-1 within three minutes when inside forward Morlock scored. Fritz Walter, playing the game of his life and moving over the sodden turf with bewildering speed, inspired them to a recovery that saw the

Germans draw level after only sixteen minutes of the game. He took a corner kick on the right, curved the ball over the Hungarian defence, and outside-right Rahn crashed it past the helpless Grosics in the Hungarian goal. The score remained 2-2 up to half-time.

In the second half, with the rain still pouring down, both teams gave it all they had. Puskas was clearly not fully fit, and his colleagues were beginning to show the rigours of their tough games against the two South American sides. With only seven minutes of the game remaining, German winger Schaefer left a tiring Bozsik in his wake and crossed the ball into the Hungarian goal area. Once again it floated tantalisingly over defenders' heads to the lurking Helmut Rahn. The big winger again crashed the ball past Grosics.

In the seven minutes that remained, the Hungarians made frantic efforts to pull the game out of the fire. The West Germans, however, were full of running to the end. As English referee Bill Ling blew the final whistle, the triumphant Germans surrounded their coach Sepp Herberger, while the Hungarians trudged disconsolately off the field.

A few minutes later, in the pouring rain, Fritz Walter accepted the trophy from Jules Rimet, the retiring head of FIFA and the man who had given his name to the World Cup. It was brought back in triumph to the West German dressing-room.

It was in the dressing-room that the post-match drama began. A short time later, when Ferenc Puskas dropped in to congratulate the Germans on their magnificent victory, he claimed he saw the entire team being violently ill. German officials said the players were suffering from jaundice, but Puskas was convinced it was the aftermath of a drug dose.

Scenting a sensational story, newsmen demanded an interview with the German team. This request was refused. As the verbal battle raged to and fro, the squad slipped quietly away. Later, Fritz Walter vigorously denied that Puskas had ever been admitted to the dressing-room.

And so the mystery remains. Did the West Germans take a stimulant before the game – or were they just too good for a Hungarian team that had played too many hard matches earlier in the tournament? And how significant a part did that tackle by Liebrich on Puskas play in the final? These are questions which often arise whenever this tournament is discussed.

Final

West Germany 3	**Hungary 2**
Morlock	Puskas
Rahn (2)	Czibor

Half-time 2-2

· SWEDEN ·

IF the World Cup matches played in Sweden lacked some of the explosive incidents that had characterised the previous finals, the tournament is remembered for putting on show a Brazil team which many soccer followers still regard as the best collection of footballers ever to grace the game.

Included in the squad was a 17-year-old wonder boy called Edson Arantes do Nascimento, better known in his home country as Pelé. Born into a poor black mining family, he was playing for the famous Santos club at 15 and when he came to Sweden he was already a Brazilian international. The youngster would be a sensation in Sweden and was destined to become the most famous footballer of all time.

Alongside Pelé in the forward line was the extraordinary 30-year-old right-winger, Garrincha. Crippled at birth, he had had to undergo innumerable operations which left him with oddly shaped knees. Nicknamed 'the Little Bird', he had overcome his childhood handicap and was now possessed of a devastating turn of speed and a rocket-like shot. The other Brazilian forwards, Didi, Vava and Zagalo, also would become household names before the World Cup was over.

Despite being able to turn out footballers of exceptional

quality, Brazil had yet to win the World Cup. There was huge pressure on coach Vincente Feola, but he had left nothing to chance this time. The training quarters outside Gothenburg had been carefully chosen months in advance and the squad's back-up staff included a doctor and a psychologist. Brazil were installed as firm favourites to win the World Cup even before they arrived in Sweden.

One man who did not fear the Brazilian maestros, however, was George Raynor. An Englishman, he was the coach and brains behind the Swedish team. Finding his services unwanted in England, he had gained coaching experience in Sweden before moving to Italy where he spent several years. He moved back to Sweden to again coach the national side for the World Cup.

What prompted him to do so was the decision by the Swedish football authorities to allow professional players into the national side. This decision opened the way for world-class players like Gunnar Gren, Kurt Hamrin and Nacka Skoglund to return from Italy and give Sweden a decent chance to win the World Cup.

Raynor watched Brazil beat Austria and the Soviet Union with ease and draw with England to head Group 4. He was impressed but not overawed. Raynor told his players: 'Take the lead against Brazil – watch them panic.' The problem was, however, that until they reached the final, no team had been able to take the lead against the brilliant Brazilians.

In the quarter-finals the Brazilians did get a bit of a shock when a gritty Welsh team, which had earlier drawn with Hungary, Mexico and Sweden, succumbed only after a shot by Pelé was deflected into the net by Welsh full-back Williams. After the game, Pelé said it was the most important goal he had ever scored.

In their quarter-final game, the Swedes came up against the Soviet Union. Urged on by their supporters, the home side played above themselves. Their diminutive right-winger Hamrin was emerging as a national hero; he tormented the Soviet defence and scored a spectacular goal in Sweden's 2-0 win. Next would come a real test, a semi-final clash with the powerful West German team. In the other semi-final, the Brazilians would meet the free-scoring French.

The Swedish-German game nearly did not take place. National fervour in Sweden was now running high and, in a bid to whip support up even further, Swedish cheerleaders were brought out onto the field before the game to ignite the huge home crowd. The German authorities were not impressed. A dispute between Swedish and German officials erupted in the stand over seating arrangements and was resolved only when the West Germans threatened to order their team from the field. Eventually the game got under way.

The Swedes started off at a furious pace and looked as if they were going to overwhelm their opponents. The Germans weathered the storm, however, and silenced the stadium by taking the lead when inside-left Hans Schaefer scored midway through the first half. Sweden equalised five minutes later when left winger Skoglund scored after the referee had turned a blind eye to a blatant handball. Early in the second half German full-back Juskowiak was sent off after he kicked Hamrin. The referee again turned a blind eye when Parling, the huge Swedish left-half, felled German captain Fritz Walter with a dreadful tackle. The veteran West German was carried off on a stretcher and when he resumed some time later he was a virtual passenger.

Sweden scored two more goals against their opponents, then playing with only nine men, thus reaching the World Cup final against the odds. The country went wild and George Raynor became the hero of the hour.

In the other semi-final, Brazil crushed France by five goals to two, with wonder-boy Pelé scoring a hat-trick. Sweden now looked to George Raynor to devise a plan to defeat Brazil in the final.

The Englishman was no fool. He knew he had worked a near miracle by getting his one-paced Swedish team to the final. He also knew they had only one chance against the brilliant Brazilians

– he would devise a plan to score an early goal, hoping the Brazilians would panic.

But the Brazilians also had an ace up their sleeve. Before the final they protested to the World Cup committee and had the Swedish cheerleaders banned from performing on the field before the game. The loss of the cheering from the terraces was a psychological blow to the Swedish team as they prepared to face the supreme test.

It made George Raynor's task that much more difficult, but just how near the unassuming Englishman came to steering his underrated outfit to glory can be gauged from the fact that, within five minutes of the start, his team took a goal lead against their fancied opponents when inside-left Nils Liedholm shot past Gilmar in Brazil's goal. It was just what George Raynor had ordered, and as the rain came down he sat back and waited for Brazil to crumble, in the manner he had predicted.

It did not happen. The *senhors* from Brazil did not get rattled. In fact they were eager for the ball to be returned to the centre spot so that they could get on with the game. On the bench, George Raynor saw this. He sensed that his plan was doomed.

It took Brazil only six minutes to equalise, and it was Garrincha who set it up. He tore down the right wing, leaving two Swedish players flat-footed, crossed the ball from the backline, and Vava swept it past goalkeeper Svensson. With just over half-an-hour gone, Garrincha again left Swedish players in his wake, hit a pinpoint ball to Vava, who beat Svensson for the second time.

Raynor tried to rally his troops at half-time, but the South Americans were about to turn on the style. Ten minutes after the interval Pelé, belying his tender years, deadened a ball with his thigh, hooked it over his head, swivelled and in one movement crashed it into the Swedish goal from twenty yards. It was a spectacular goal and the packed stadium cheered him to the echo.

Pelé was simply magnificent. He roamed the field, spraying accurate passes to Vava, Didi, Zagalo and Garrincha, his colleagues in a Brazilian forward line that tore holes in the Swedish defence. With thirteen minutes remaining, left-winger Zagalo sped past two defenders and scored a fourth Brazilian goal. He fell to his knees and wept tears of joy. The prize was almost theirs at last.

From the packed terraces the drums began to beat and cries of 'Samba, Samba' went up from the delighted Brazilian followers. They were stifled momentarily a few minutes later when Agne Simonsson got Sweden's second goal. But before the end Pelé rose magnificently to head a cross from Zagalo past a frustrated Svensson. Five goals to two – and Brazil at last had won the Jules Rimet trophy.

Several of the Brazilian players were so overcome with emotion that it was some time before they recovered sufficiently to join their team-mates in a lap of honour. They danced around like excited children, holding aloft first their own flag, then Sweden's. The home crowd, though disappointed, rose to their feet. No one could dispute that the better team had won.

Teenager Pelé would go on to star in three more World Cups for Brazil and create football history by playing for his home club, Santos, for almost twenty years. But in Sweden the unsung hero remained the unassuming Englishman George Raynor. He had brought an unfancied Swedish team to the brink of glory. Yet just over a year previously he had been forced to quit England – because no team there considered him good enough to be offered a job as coach.

Final

Sweden 2	**Brazil 5**
Liedholm	Vava (2)
Simonsson	Pelé (2)
	Zagalo

Half-time 1-2

· CHILE ·

WHEN the members of FIFA decided to designate Chile as the country to host the 1962 World Cup, there were misgivings among several of the European nations which had qualified for the finals. They were apprehensive that an impoverished country like Chile would not do justice to such an important tournament, and they pointed to the vast distances that teams in the various groups would have to travel in a country like Chile.

The fact that a couple of earthquakes had devastated much of the country during the discussions on where the World Cup should be held did not exactly help the Chilean cause. But when it was pointed out at the FIFA Congress in 1960 that the previous two tournaments had been held in Europe, it was obvious that Chile would win the day.

In the final analysis Chile won the vote over Argentina, and work began on the building of a new stadium in Santiago where the final would take place. The fact that a quartet of teams in one of the four groups would play their games thousands of miles away in the northern city of Arica, near the Peruvian border, was conveniently overlooked.

England was in Group 4 with Bulgaria, Argentina and Hungary, with the teams playing their games in a stadium owned by a local copper company in the run-down, seedy city of Rancagua. Brazil, World Cup champions and favourites to win again, were happy to be drawn in the group that would play their matches on the coast at Viña del Mar. The host country was conveniently based in Santiago where they were assured of hysterical home support against the European trio of Italy, West Germany and Switzerland.

If Brazil were favourites to win the Jules Rimet trophy for a second time in succession, there was one European side which the experts reckoned would provide stiff opposition.

That team was the Soviet Union. They had prepared thoroughly for the World Cup, bringing their squad on a hugely successful South American tour the year previously, during which they had defeated Argentina, Uruguay and Chile. Back again for the World Cup, they were expected to advance easily from the group that would play in far-off Arica which included Yugoslavia, Colombia, and old rivals Uruguay.

What the Soviets did not reckon with was the inexplicable loss of form in the tournament of Lev Yashin, their giant goalkeeper and, they reckoned, the best custodian in the world. Moscow-born Yashin had first played for his country in 1954 and had quickly established himself as one of the all-time greats of Soviet sport. With him as the last line of defence, the Soviet goal was almost impregnable. In his customary all-black strip, the towering Yashin was a formidable figure, whose uncanny positional sense, sharp reflexes and cat-like agility made him very difficult to beat.

How then, does one explain the great Yashin having to pick the ball out of his net four times in the Soviets' second game against the no-hopers of Colombia? In the first game the Soviets had beaten a useful Yugoslavian side 2-0, and they were expected to romp home against Colombia. With the score 4-1 they were doing that when Yashin made a bad mistake and was beaten directly from a corner kick. Then, in the last quarter of the game he let in two more goals.

His display prompted one French reporter to predict that it was the beginning of the end for the world's No. 1 goalkeeper, a man who had been honoured with the Order of Lenin and Master of Sport awards. In the Soviets' final group game against Uruguay, Yashin again failed to keep a clean sheet, although his side won 2-1 and qualified to face Chile in the quarter-final.

The tournament had now reached the knock-out stage. In the vital game against Chile, the great Lev Yashin blundered twice and was responsible for his team making an early return home. He failed to save a 25-yard free-kick when the game was only ten minutes old, and he committed an even bigger mistake later in the first half when he let a 35-yard shot from Chilean half-back Rojas fly past him into the net. Yashin's team-mates looked on in disbelief.

Meanwhile the host country were cock-a-hoop. Against all the odds they had reached the semi-final, thanks to earlier victories over Switzerland and Italy. The win against the Italians was particularly welcome; before the tournament began, Italian journalists had ridiculed the country and made remarks about Chilean women. It had angered the nation.

When the two teams met in Santiago, the home crowd roared for Italian blood. They got it when the referee's back was turned and a Chilean player broke Italian defender Maschio's nose with a punch. The Chileans constantly spat at the Italians during the game, but incredibly the English referee sent off two Italians! Not surprisingly, Chile won 2-0.

Champions Brazil were also having their problems. They lost their hero Pelé in their second game against Czechoslovakia when he pulled a thigh muscle. Pelé took no further part in the tournament and his place was taken by a virtual unknown called Amarildo.

Amarildo seized his opportunity with both feet. The youngster was not overawed in joining a forward line that included legendary names like Garrincha, Vava and Didi. And he proved it in the vital third game against Spain when, with the World Cup favourites 1-0 down and struggling, Amarildo equalised with a swerving shot. Towards the end of a pulsating encounter, he popped up to head home a Garrincha cross and ensured Brazil's passage to the next round.

Hosting the World Cup seems to inspire home nations, and Chile in 1962 was no exception. They began as outsiders among the sixteen teams in the finals, but when the smoke of the earlier games, had cleared, Chile were in the semi-finals with soccer giants Brazil, Czechoslovakia and Yugoslavia. Up and down the length of the thin strip of country, the populace went soccer crazy. Everyone dreamed of World Cup glory.

The brilliance of the Brazilians shattered that dream, however. In a tempestuous battle in a packed Santiago stadium, Garrincha scored for the champions after only nine minutes with one of his left-foot specials. With just over half-an-hour gone, he climbed high to head a centre from Zagalo past Escutti in the Chilean goal. But as half-time approached, the Santiago stadium erupted when midfielder Toro pulled one back for Chile.

It was 2-1 to Brazil at the interval. The game had barely restarted when Garrincha sent over a corner and Vava scored for Brazil. Still Chile were not finished. Under pressure, Brazilian defender Zozimo handled the ball and Sanchez scored from the penalty. At 3-2, Brazil kept their composure and Vava assured them of a place in the final when he headed his second goal from a cross by Zagalo.

The excitement still was not over. Before the end of the game, Garrincha was sent off for punching an opponent. As he walked to the dressing-room, he was hit on the head by a flying bottle. Chilean centre-forward Landa was also given his marching orders before the final whistle.

In the final, Brazil would face the solid, unspectacular Czechoslovakians, the surprise packet of the tournament. Not rated when the finals began, the strong, methodical Czechs, relying mainly on a sturdy defence that never panicked under pressure, had scored a mere three goals in the opening four games, which included a scoreless draw against Brazil.

In the semi-final against the fancied Yugoslavia they had triumphed by 3-1. The man the Czechs had to thank for getting to the final was goalkeeper Dimitri Schroiff. He had displayed outstanding form in the tournament thus far, and his team-mates were banking on him doing the same against Brazil's deadly marksmen Garrincha, Vava and Amarildo in the final.

But to everyone's amazement, Schroiff lost his nerve and cost Czechoslovakia the World Cup. Like the great Lev Yashin earlier, the so-dependable Schroiff suffered an inexplicable loss of form in the most important game of his life.

And yet it could have been so different for the underdogs.

Although Brazil were overwhelming favourites to win, the Czechs shrugged off the tag of no-hopers and in the early stages came out of their defensive shell to play neat, attacking football. In the sixteenth minute they stunned the crowd, and the Brazilians, by scoring an opportunist goal.

Inside-forward Scherer received the ball in midfield, saw Masopust begin a run through the middle, and floated the ball over the Brazilian defence. Masopust controlled the ball beautifully before crashing a left-foot shot past Gilmar in the Brazilian goal.

That goal could have spurred Czechoslovakia to victory, but Schroiff made his first mistake shortly afterwards when, in Brazil's next attack, Amarildo advanced with the ball along the left goal line. A score looked almost impossible from such an acute angle, but Schroiff left a gap and Amarildo curled a shot around him and into the net.

The writing was on the wall for the Czechs after that error. Halfway through the second half Amarildo again demonstrated his genius by making space for himself on the wing and crossing the ball. Schroiff was badly positioned and Zito had no trouble heading into goal.

Poor Schroiff! He committed a third error sixteen minutes from full-time when Brazilian full-back Djalma Santos lashed a high ball hopefully into the Czech penalty area. Schroiff later claimed that it went against the sun, dazzling him. He allowed the ball to slip from his grasp and Vava had the simple task of side-footing it over the goal line.

Brazil were once again World Cup champions. And two of the world's top goalkeepers, Lev Yashin and Dimitri Schroiff, left Chile with a nightmare of memories. For Yashin at least there was life after Chile – he was voted European Player of the Year the following season.

Final

Brazil 3	**Czechoslovakia 1**
Amarildo	Masopust
Zito	
Vava	

Half-time 1-1

· ENGLAND (1) ·

THEY came to England for the 1966 World Cup without an earthly chance of winning the famous trophy. Indeed, some commentators said openly that the North Koreans had no right to be in the finals. But by the time the team left Britain they had the fans singing their praises – and they would provide enough shocks to make the soccer world sit up and take notice.

The outcry against the little men from Korea playing in the 1966 finals began even before they had left home. After all, they had had to beat only one team, Australia, to book their tickets to Britain from the Afro-Asia group.

That extraordinary situation had come about because the other seventeen teams in Afro-Asia, angry that only one team would qualify from the group, had pulled out of the qualifying stages in protest. That left the unknown, inexperienced North Koreans and an Australian team, equally inexperienced but boosted by immigrants from soccer-playing countries like England and Italy. Australia were expected to see off the Koreans in the two qualifying games.

The two games were played on neutral territory at Phnom-Penh in Cambodia. The North Koreans had been taken away to a camp for several weeks for rigorous training and it showed. In the first game they displayed excellent teamwork and extraordinary dexterity, allied to deadly finishing, to crush the Australians by six goals to nil. They won the second game, easing up, by three goals to one.

With their place in the World Cup finals assured, the North Koreans went back into training and into obscurity. When they arrived in England a few months later, the focus of the media was not on their soccer skills, but on tongue-twisting team members' names like O Yoon Kyung, Han Bong Jin and Yang Sung Kook.

The North Koreans faced an awesome array of talent in Britain. Among the national soccer giants who had qualified for the 1966 World Cup finals were the holders, the brilliant Brazilians; Portugal, with ace goal poacher Eusebio, known as the Black Panther; Italy, already twice winners of the Jules Rimet trophy; and Argentina, led by iron man and captain Antonio Rattin.

The sixteen teams were split into four groups, with two from each to qualify for the quarter-finals. When the North Koreans were drawn in Group 4, a section that included the powerful Soviet Union, Italy and Chile, it looked as if they would be catching an early plane home.

The Group 4 games were played in the soccer-mad North-East of England where the Geordie fans took the North Korean underdogs to their hearts. Despite vociferous support, however, the muscular Soviets brushed aside the Koreans' skilful challenge in the opening game, winning 3-0. In their second game the Koreans had a commendable 1-1 draw with Chile. The Soviets also defeated Italy, who had beaten Chile in their opening game. If in the final games the USSR, the favourites, beat Chile, this meant that Italy would need only to draw with the North Koreans to advance to the next round. It looked to be a foregone conclusion.

All was not well in the Italian camp, however. The nation that had won the World Cup on two previous occasions was having a crisis of confidence. Manager Edmondo Fabbri was chopping and changing the team; a couple of their top players were injured, while others were squabbling. There were angry rumblings back home at the team's performance. Fear of losing to the tournament minnows and going home in disgrace haunted the players.

The game was played in Ayrsome Park, Middlesbrough and the fans, sensing an upset, got solidly behind the North Koreans. Italy began tentatively and it was obvious that some of the players were having difficulty coping with the speed of the more lightly built Koreans. Their cause was not helped when defender Bulgarelli injured himself in a blatant foul tackle after thirty minutes and had to go off.

'Ko-re-a! Ko-re-a!' chanted the Middlesbrough crowd as the Koreans teased and tormented the Italians with their skilful play. And then, just before half-time, the North Koreans scored!

In the forty-second minute little inside-left Pak Doo Ik won the ball in a tackle, bore down on the Italian goal, and crashed a cross shot past the advancing Italian goalkeeper, Albertosi. The crowd went wild.

At half-time the Koreans trooped off to a standing ovation. Meanwhile, word was being flashed all around the world that a stunning upset was on the cards. In Italy, the tide of anger mounted.

In the second half the Koreans, far from being overawed, gave as good as they got. Their trainer rightly reckoned that if his players went back into defence and tried to hold onto their slender lead, the more physically powerful Italians would overwhelm them. He urged his team to attack.

The Koreans did not score again, but their non-stop aggression prevented the Italians from putting the ball in the net. When the referee blew the final whistle, the Middlesbrough crowd spilled over the barriers and carried the Koreans off shoulder-high. The Italians slunk off dejectedly, fearful of what lay ahead when they returned home.

The Soviets beat Chile by 2-1 in Roker Park, Sunderland, which meant that the North Koreans had advanced to the last eight of the World Cup where they would have another glory day against Portugal. Suddenly the soccer writers were having to become familiar with those almost unpronounceable three-pronged names!

While the Koreans prepared for their quarter-final clash with Portugal, the Italians were returning home in disgrace. Fearful of the reception awaiting them, manager Fabbri and his team flew into Genoa airport in the dead of night. It did not save them from the wrath of the hundreds of angry fans who were there to meet them. Rotten fruit, eggs and jeers rained down in abundance from a crowd who had hoped to see their team return with a third World Cup. In the investigation that followed, Edmondo Fabbri was fired.

For sheer drama, the Portugal versus North Korean game in Goodison Park, Liverpool would be hard to beat. By now nobody, least of all the Portuguese, were taking the little Asians lightly. There was a sensational opening when the Koreans swept into the attack and midfielder Pak Seung Jin scored in the first minute.

They had more to cheer about when diminutive inside-left Li Dong Woon danced through a bemused Portuguese defence and scored a second goal twenty minutes later. The crowd could scarcely believe its eyes two minutes later when outside-left Yang Sung Kook crashed in a third. An upset of monumental proportions was on the cards!

But it was not to be. The great Eusebio pulled Portugal together and triggered off a marvellous escape act. He was all over the field, jinking, turning and flashing shots at Li Chan Myung in the Korean goal. The Black Panther pulled a goal back in the twenty-eighth minute and scored a second from a penalty before half-time when his team-mate, inside-left Torres, was felled near goal.

Fifteen minutes into the second half and it was Eusebio again, equalising after a dazzling dribble through the Korean defence. The Asians were battling gamely, but they had no answer to Eusebio. He was tearing through again when he was fouled. He recovered to crash in the penalty – he had scored four goals in a 35-minute spell and had put Portugal in front. A short while later inside-right José Augusto scored a fifth and it was all over for North Korea.

The unknowns left the World Cup stage to a standing ovation from a crowd who had admired their skills and had delighted in the entertainment. The North Koreans had arrived in Britain as no-hopers, but left as heroes. The home team, England, would garner its share of headlines in the 1966 World Cup. But soccer fans everywhere would also remember the exploits of the men from Asia.

· ENGLAND (2) ·

THE pundits did not exactly laugh outright when, not long after he was appointed England manager in 1963, Alf Ramsey promised the nation that his team would win the 1966 World Cup. And that possibility looked even less likely when, in their first match under Ramsey's command, the England team were soundly beaten 5-2 by France in Paris.

True, the World Cup would be held in England in 1966, but no home team had won the coveted trophy since Italy in 1934. And when the England team kicked off the tournament with a dour, scoreless draw against Uruguay in London's Wembley Stadium, the pundits shook their heads and looked elsewhere for a possible winner.

Whatever Alf Ramsey's thoughts were as he saw his team struggle to score against the Uruguayans, they could not be gauged from the inscrutable look on his face as he sat on the bench. As sole selector, a condition he had insisted on with the English Football Association before he accepted the post of team manager, Ramsey knew his reputation was on the line. One of his most daring gambits was to field a team without recognised wingers in a 4-3-3 formation.

He relied on his pacey full-backs, George Cohen and Ray

Wilson, to overlap down the wing and cross the ball into the opponents' penalty area where goal-grabbers Jimmy Greaves and Roger Hunt were lurking. The balding Bobby Charlton in midfield was also a constant threat with his thundering shots from far out.

It was a unique formation, one that had never been tried before and which, in due course, would change the face of soccer. However, after that less than successful joust against the rugged Uruguayans in the opening game, Ramsey's odd-looking team was dismissed as serious contenders for World Cup honours.

The opinions of the critics and the soccer writers mattered little to Alf Ramsey. He had a World Cup campaign planned for his English team and, whether the fans and the soccer writers liked it or not, he was going to stick by that plan. It was not the first time in a career as a player and manager that he had faced criticism; he was never afraid to make unpopular decisions and he would do so again during this World Cup.

As a player he had had to live down the stigma of being a member of the England team that had been sensationally defeated by outsiders, the United States, in the 1950 World Cup in Brazil. Small and sturdy in stature, Ramsey was an intelligent player and had enjoyed a distinguished career as full-back with London's fashionable and very successful club Tottenham Hotspur. When his playing days were over, he had been appointed manager of the hard-up Third Division side Ipswich Town. Under Ramsey's astute managership, the unfashionable little club had won promotion to do battle with the giants of the First Division.

After the 1962 World Cup, when the English Football Association was seeking its first ever full-time manager, they picked Alf Ramsey. He came on his own terms, and with the avowed intention of winning the trophy when it would be played on home territory four years later.

Recognised as something of a martinet, he nevertheless had

the full confidence and trust of his players. Chief among those was half-back Bobby Moore, a prince among footballers and a captain who would carry out Ramsey's instructions to the letter on the field. Two of Ramsey's more unorthodox choices for his World Cup squad were the Leeds United veteran Jack Charlton, an ex-miner and uncompromising centre-half, and Nobby Stiles of Manchester United, a midfielder who lacked finesse, but who tackled like a terrier and whose gap-toothed visage gave him a fearsome appearance.

Of the sixteen teams who came to England for the 1966 World Cup finals, the Brazilians, with the great Pelé still a potent force in this, his third World Cup, were the favourites. The *senhors* from South America had won the 1958 and 1962 tournaments and came to Europe determined to make it a hat-trick of victories. Argentina, Italy and West Germany were also reckoned to be in with a good chance of lifting the trophy.

Of the European teams it was reckoned that, while England with home advantage could not be discounted, both Hungary and Portugal had players who were capable of winning the World Cup. If Brazil had the incomparable Pelé, Portugal had in their squad a black pearl from Mozambique called Eusebio, a centre forward of immense talent and goal-scoring ability. Eusebio would emerge as one of the stars of the 1966 World Cup.

It was unfortunate that Brazil, Hungary and Portugal were all drawn together in Group 3, along with Bulgaria. With only two teams advancing to the next round, it meant that one of the pre-tournament favourites would make an early exit. It turned out to be Brazil, who beat Bulgaria 2-0 in their opening match at Goodison Park, but then went down 3-1 to the brilliant Hungarians in a breathtaking game a few days later. Pelé, injured in that first game, came back for the vital match against Portugal, but he was clearly unfit. A crunching tackle midway through the first half had Pelé vowing that he would never play in another World Cup. Eusebio scored twice in Portugal's 3-1 win and, with Hungary defeating Bulgaria in their final game in the group, it was Brazil's footballers who took an early plane home to Rio.

Meanwhile, Alf Ramsey's English squad did all that was expected of them, without looking world beaters. They had their first win when they beat Mexico 2-0, then had an unremarkable 2-0 victory over France. They finished top of Group 1, ahead of Uruguay, to advance to the quarter-finals. Ramsey knew changes would have to be made if his team was to fulfil his prophecy of winning the trophy.

For the quarter-final clash against the rugged Argentinians at Wembley, destined to enter the annals of soccer for all the wrong reasons, the English manager boldly introduced Geoff Hurst at inside-right instead of the goal-poaching Jimmy Greaves, who was injured. It was a switch which, in retrospect, would set England on the path to World Cup glory.

The game had hardly begun when the tough-tackling Argentinians were committing a string of fouls, and having their names inscribed in the German referee's notebook. Chief culprit was the towering Argentinian centre-half and captain, Antonio Rattin. His was an intimidating figure, fouling, gesticulating, arguing every decision with the referee.

Ten minutes before half-time the German official had had enough. Rattin was disputing another decision when the official pointed to the sideline. The Argentinian captain was being ordered off – but he refused to go! It took eight minutes of cajoling before the scowling Argentinian was persuaded to obey the referee's ruling. The incident was to sour relationships between the football authorities in Europe and South America.

Reduced to ten men, the Argentinians battled valiantly. But with just thirteen minutes to go, England scored – Geoff

Hurst getting the all-important goal. Ramsey's men were now into the semi-final and the players were gaining in confidence. Fervour was running high and the fans got right behind their team. Perhaps Alf Ramsey was right: maybe their team could win the World Cup!

First, they would have to overcome a Portuguese team, brilliantly lead by Eusebio, which had already beaten Brazil and Hungary and which, in a very exciting quarter-final, had come from three goals down to beat surprise packets North Korea by 5-3. Ramsey knew it would be a tough match, but he was confident England could fulfill his prediction and win the World Cup.

Wembley Stadium was packed to capacity for the semi-final. For days before the kick-off, speculation had raged in the media and among the fans about the composition of Alf Ramsey's line-up. Would he retain the hard-working Geoff Hurst of West Ham in the forward line, or would he bring back goal-grabber Jimmy Greaves of Tottenham Hotspur, the fans' favourite and a skilful player, but one whom Ramsey felt did not pull his weight during the full ninety minutes? In the event Ramsey, always his own man, went against popular opinion and selected Hurst.

The ungainly Nobby Stiles was another player whom Ramsey took a chance on for the vital game against Portugal. The English manager had delegated Stiles to take on the unenviable job of nullifying the mercurial Eusebio. The purists felt that the job of marking Eusebio, the tournament's leading goal-scorer, would be beyond Stiles.

It turned out to be another Ramsey masterstroke. In a splendid encounter, full of flowing football and breathtaking incidents, the English players scaled heights the likes of which their fanatical fans had never thought possible. And the hero of the hour was none other than the short-sighted Nobby Stiles, who wore contact lenses during the game and who made sure that the great Eusebio hardly got a touch of the ball!

Not only did Nobby overshadow the great Portuguese forward, but he also found time to harangue his team-mates and encourage them to greater effort. And not far behind him was Jack Charlton, the towering Geordie who, in the 1990s, would, as manager, lead the Republic of Ireland to two World Cup finals. Two thundering goals by Jack's brother Bobby, to a late goal scored by Eusebio from a penalty, set the seal on a famous victory. In the final England would meet West Germany, who had defeated the Soviet Union by the same score in the other semi-final.

Once more Alf Ramsey came in for a storm of criticism when he announced the English team for the final. Geoff Hurst was again in instead of Jimmy Greaves. To the pundits, it seemed crazy to leave a goal-grabber like Greaves on the bench for such an historic encounter. Even though Hurst had played extremely well since he had come into the team, the pressure was on Ramsey to drop either him or the other inside-forward, Liverpool's Roger Hunt.

But it was Alf Ramsey who had the last laugh. In an exciting final, which England won 4-2 and which went into extra-time when the West Germans scored an equaliser in the last minute of normal time, Geoff Hurst scored three goals and became the first man ever to score a hat-trick in a World Cup final. His West Ham colleague, Martin Peters, had put England 2-1 ahead with an opportunist goal with only twelve minutes of ordinary time remaining.

Hurst, however, was the real hero for England scoring a goal which even today is a source of controversy and which everyone in West Germany is still convinced should not have been given. It happened in the first period of extra-time when winger Alan Ball sent over a cross into the German penalty area and Hurst hit it on the volley. The ball cannoned off the underside of the

German crossbar and bounced down. After consultation with his linesman, the Swiss referee signalled a goal. It left England leading 3-2 and, in the last minute of the second period of extra-time, Hurst scored again to leave England clear winners.

As the referee signalled the end, the exhausted World Cup champions surrounded their team manager. They knew that the self-belief which Alf Ramsey had instilled in the team had been vital to victory. Nobby Stiles unashamedly shed tears and wiped them away with a sweat-stained jersey. In time, Alf Ramsey would become a national hero and receive a knighthood. More important, against the odds he had made his prediction of four years before come true.

Final

England 4	**West Germany 2**
Hurst (3)	Haller
Peters	Weber

(after extra-time)

Half-time 1-1 Full-time 2-2

· MEXICO ·

BY the time four of the world's strongest teams had battled through to the semi-finals of the 1970 World Cup, an intriguing situation had developed. Three of the four teams – Uruguay, Italy and Brazil – had won the trophy on two previous occasions; were either of them to triumph again, that nation would keep the trophy for all time.

The other semi-finalist was West Germany, who four years earlier had been beaten in the final against England at Wembley. West Germany had won the trophy once before, in 1954, and were confident they could triumph again in Mexico.

World champions England had arrived in Mexico, also confident of retaining the title, but their chances of doing so were diminished somewhat by the attitude of team manager Sir Alf Ramsey, hero of the 1966 win. His brusque manner rubbed the Mexican hosts up the wrong way, causing unnecessary difficulty for his players. Sir Alf would also be guilty of a tactical error in the quarter-final game against West Germany which would lead to England being eliminated from the tournament.

In fact, it seemed there was a conspiracy afoot to make sure that England would not win the World Cup in Mexico. How can one explain the extraordinary incident that saw England captain,

Bobby Moore, being accused, arrested and jailed for allegedly stealing a diamond necklace from a jeweller's shop in the team's hotel?

This unsavoury incident happened after the English squad had arrived in Mexico, a month in advance of the World Cup finals, in order to acclimatise themselves to the extremes of heat and altitude. Having settled into their training quarters, they then left Mexico to play two friendly games in Colombia and Equador. It was after these games, on a stop-over in Bogotá on the way back to Mexico, that England's captain was accused of stealing a bracelet from the jewellers in the hotel where the team was staying.

It was an outrageous charge and one which faded into oblivion after the man who had made the accusation mysteriously disappeared. The English team returned to Mexico without Moore, who joined them a few days later after being released from jail.

Despite the upset, England qualified for the quarter-finals, defeating Romania and Czechoslovakia, and losing only 1-0 to a Brazilian team that was already looking like champions. In the quarter-finals, however, England lost 3-2 to West Germany, despite leading 2-0 with only forty minutes to go.

It was shortly after this that Sir Alf, the man who had made England world champions four years before, made what many still consider a fatal tactical error. With his team performing splendidly in the searing heat of Leon, he took off midfielders Martin Peters and the peerless Bobby Charlton, replacing them with Colin Bell and Norman Hunter.

Just before Ramsey had taken Charlton off, admittedly, West Germany's elegant captain, Franz Beckenbauer, had pulled a goal back. The Germans had feared Charlton's explosive shooting, and Beckenbauer's job was to shadow Charlton everywhere.

When Sir Alf substituted Charlton, it freed Beckenbauer to come forward and play a more attacking game. He immediately began to cause chaos in the English defence, and played a major part in helping his team score two further goals which eliminated England.

In the semi-finals, defence-conscious Italy surprised many by defeating the West Germans in a high-scoring game by four goals to three. In the other semi-final, Brazil, with a magnificent team that included names like Rivelino, Jairzinho and Pelé, the latter still only 29 years old but already a veteran of four World Cups, easily defeated old rivals Uruguay by three goals to one.

So it was a classic World Cup final confrontation – a European team clashing with one from South America for the honour of keeping soccer's most coveted trophy. The tough-tackling Italians were confident their defence would shut out the brilliant Brazilians and stifle the samba beat on the terraces. The plan then would be for ace goal poacher Luigi Riva to score on the break, and to mount a ten-man defence to the final whistle. It was a sterile approach by Italian trainer Valcareggi, compared to the all-out-attack policy of Brazil.

The one chink in the Brazilian armour was Felix, their goalkeeper. Not very tall, he was prone to high balls and had an unpredictable streak. Could the Italians cash in on his vulnerability?

This was to be the great Pelé's farewell to international football. Exactly twelve years and one week to the day the teenage Edson Arantes do Nascimento had made his World Cup debut in Sweden. Brazil had won the final that year and Pelé had scored two excellent goals. Could he do the same in the Azteca Stadium in Mexico City?

The Brazilians took the lead within eighteen minutes. Rivelino crossed a ball into the centre and the majestic Pelé rose high above the Italian defenders and sent a powerful downward header past goalkeeper Albertosi. Green and gold banners waved aloft on the terraces and the samba drums echoed around the stadium.

The Italians were hard-pressed not to concede another goal to the rampant Brazilians. They held out, and created a few chances themselves through the brilliance of veteran forwards Sandrino Mazzola and Gianni Rivera. They battled their way back into the game and scored when a careless back-heel by Brazilian Clodoaldo was picked up by Boninsegna. He raced through the Brazilian defence, rounded Felix, and slotted the ball into the unguarded net.

The score remained 1-1 at half-time. The advantage had swung Italy's way, but unfortunately they did not seize it. Instead of throwing caution to the winds and attacking Brazil, they resorted to negative football again and tried to close up the game. Pelé and his team-mates regained their rhythm and powered forward, hardly able to believe their luck.

Pelé was magnificent. He controlled the tempo of the game, his deft touches varying from short passes to long balls that found a colleague with pinpoint accuracy. He rode some heavy tackles and never lost his cool as the Italian defenders resorted to petty fouls in their desperation to stifle his talent.

The samba beat rose to a crescendo in the sixty-sixth minute when midfielder Gerson hit a tremendous left-foot shot that fairly screamed into the Italian net. Five minutes later Gerson took a free kick which Pelé, with the gentlest of touches, diverted into the path of the on-rushing Jairzinho. With Facchetti, his marker, floundering in his wake, Jairzinho slid the ball past the diving Albertosi.

The score was now 3-1 and Italy were a well-beaten side. They battled gamely, but the fluency of the Brazilians was too much for them. With only three minutes to go, they set up another blistering attack. This time it was Jairzinho who found Pelé with a long pass. Controlling it in one smooth movement, the mesmerised Italian defenders could only watch as Pelé nonchalantly stroked the ball into the path of full-back Carlos Alberto, who had come thundering up behind him. Another cannonball of a shot, and poor Albertosi was picking the ball out of his net for the fourth time.

Joyous scenes greeted the final whistle. Thousands of ecstatic Brazilian fans poured onto the pitch and turned the Azteca Stadium into a sea of waving green and gold banners. They surrounded their heroes, the players were hoisted shoulder-high and carried around amid scenes of high emotion.

Pelé was the main focus for much of the exuberance; when he climbed the stairway to claim his third World Cup medal and waved to the crowd, the cheering was deafening.

Brazil had created soccer history and it was fitting that the Jules Rimet trophy should find its final resting place in a country which believed in total football, played with the skill and verve of true masters. In the van of that movement was the incomparable Pelé, now retired from the world stage. In West Germany four years hence, the nations would compete for a new trophy, to be known simply as the World Cup. The name of Jules Rimet, however, would be remembered for all time as the man who, four decades before, had set in motion this great tournament.

Final

Brazil 4	**Italy 1**
Pelé	Boninsegna
Gerson	
Jairzinho	
Carlos Alberto	

Half-time 1-1

Eusebio of Portugal is stopped by North Korea's Shin Yung Kyoo and goalkeeper Ri Chan Myung in the quarter-final clash at Goodison Park during the 1966 World Cup finals.

Portugal's Augusto heads goal number five past North Korea's goalkeeper Ri Chan Myung in the 1966 finals. (Popperfoto)

England's Jack Charlton tackles West Germany's Held in the 1966 final. (Popperfoto)

Bobby Charlton kneels in the German goalmouth after a near miss during the 1966 final.

West Germany's Haller (out of shot) beats England goalkeeper Gordon Banks to score the first German goal in the 1966 final at Wembley. (Popperfoto)

The last minute equaliser. Thirty seconds to go in the 1966 World Cup final and West Germany's Weber sidefoots the ball past England's goalkeeper Banks, to snatch the equaliser at Wembley to bring the game into extra-time. Also included are (l-r) Seeler, Cohen, Moore, Wilson and Schnellinger (white shirt). Background (extreme right) Jack Charlton. (Popperfoto)

England's Jack Charlton falls to his knees in relief as colleagues Hurst and Peters celebrate in the background after the 1966 final.

England captain Bobby Moore holds the World Cup aloft as his team-mates carry him around Wembley after the 1966 final. (Popperfoto)

Pelé turns away in triumph after scoring Brazil's first goal against Italy in the final of the 1970 World Cup in Mexico. (Colorsport)

Brazil's Jairzinho causes problems for Italian goalkeeper Albertosi and defender Facchetti in the 1970 final in Mexico City. (Popperfoto)

Gerry Armstrong of Northern Ireland blasts the ball past Spanish goalkeeper Arconada in Valencia in his side's surprise 1-0 win during the 1982 World Cup finals. (Colorsport)

England's Bryan Robson shoots past French goalkeeper Jean Luc Ettori to score the fastest goal in the World Cup finals – just 27 seconds after the kick-off in the first round of the 1982 World Cup in Bilbao.

West Germany's goalkeeper Harald Schumacher walks away after felling France's Patrick Battiston in a torrid encounter in Seville during the 1982 World Cup finals. Amazingly Schumacher was not sent off for the blatant foul and West Germany went on to win the game in an extra-time penalty shoot-out. (Colorsport)

Italy's Dino Zoff stretches to save during the 1982 World Cup final against West Germany.

Paolo Rossi, goal-scoring hero of Italy's World Cup win in Spain in 1982, does it again against West Germany in the final. (Colorsport)

Diego Maradona raises the World Cup aloft after Argentina had beaten West Germany 3-2 in the 1986 World Cup in Mexico.

English players protest after Diego Maradona's 'Hand of God' goal had put Argentina 1-0 ahead in the Azteca Stadium during the 1986 World Cup finals in Mexico. (Sporting Pictures)

Karl-Heinz Rummenigge of West Germany and Patrick Battiston of France in a battle for possession during the 1986 World Cup.

A tense moment in the Italy vs Bulgaria tie during the 1986 finals as the Italians prepare to take a free kick close to the Bulgarian goal. (Sporting Pictures)

Irish goalkeeper Packie Bonner makes the vital fifth penalty save against Romania in Genoa which put the Republic of Ireland into the last eight of the 1990 World Cup in Italy. (Irish Press)

Ekeke of Cameroon scores his side's second goal against England in the quarter-finals of the 1990 World Cup.

Maradona of Argentina and Buchwald of West Germany at close quarters in the final of the 1990 World Cup. It was probably the worst final ever in the tournament's history. (Sporting Pictures)

The goal that won it for West Germany... Andreas Brehme scores after his side had been awarded a doubtful penalty late in the 1990 final against Argentina. (Sporting Pictures)

West German players celebrate after winning the 1990 World Cup in Rome against Argentina. (Sporting Pictures)

1974

· WEST GERMANY ·

THE World Cup was held in West Germany for the first time in 1974, exactly twenty years after they had won the trophy with that stunning victory over favourites Hungary in Berne. Who would grab centre stage and light up the tournament as Pelé had done in the past? That question was a topic of discussion as the sixteen nations which had qualified for Germany prepared to battle it out in the finals.

Brazil was not only without the gifted Pelé, who despite pleadings from his fans adamantly refused to play in another World Cup, but the team also had to travel to Europe to defend the title without other great players like midfielders Tostao and Gerson, also Clodoaldo, a forward with dazzling pace and a bullet shot.

While Tostao, Gerson and Clodoaldo had been ruled out through injury, Pelé, still only 32, decided that he had been the victim of too many scything tackles from unscrupulous defenders over the years. And so the spotlight switched to Europe, and to Johan Cruyff of Holland and Franz Beckenbauer of West Germany, two scintillating players whose football skills and deadly rivalry would dominate the tournament and who were destined to clash in what would be a final worthy of the occasion.

Holland had a team that bristled with talent. Apart from Cruyff, it contained names like gifted midfielder Arie Haan, the livewire winger Johnny Rep, and the multi-talented Johann Neeskens. Veteran Jan Jongbloed was the third choice goalkeeper who was recalled to duty when injury eliminated Van Beveren and Schrijvers, the first two choices for net minder; in true fairytale fashion Jongbloed became one of Holland's heroes and was influential in getting the Dutch to their first ever World Cup final.

But the man who really inspired Holland was Johan Cruyff, the 27-year-old who had joined crack team Ajax as a 10-year-old schoolboy and who had just been named European Footballer of the Year for a record third time. He had speed, great ball control, uncanny positional sense and a deadly shot in either foot.

West Germany also had its stars, none more so than the elegant Franz Beckenbauer in midfield, playing in his third World Cup and still chasing a winning medal. He was a dominating figure who could control a game, covering in defence while at the same time hitting pinpoint passes, and he was exceptional at darting through from midfield to score important goals.

The hope among rival fans was that West Germany and Holland would avoid each other in the early games and would clash in the final, when the duel between the mercurial Cruyff and his great rival, Beckenbauer, with the greatest soccer prize of all at stake, would surely be one to behold.

The eagerly awaited final between the two superpowers of European soccer almost did not happen. Once again the men who control the World Cup, anxious to ensure that the two best teams reached the final, ordained that the sixteen teams which had qualified for West Germany would be split into four groups. After eight of these had been eliminated, the remaining eight would again be split into groups of four. After a further series of games, the two teams heading each group would qualify for the final.

When it came to the quarter finals, the Dutch found themselves in Group A with favourites Brazil, the solid East Germans and the unpredictable Argentinians. By contrast, West Germany was in the easier all-European Group B, which comprised Yugoslavia, Sweden and Poland.

In Gelsenkirchen, Holland gave notice that they were the team of the tournament when, in the opening game in their group, they overwhelmed Argentina by 4-0. The Dutch were brilliant, from the rejuvenated Jongbloed, blossoming as the stand-in goalkeeper, to the excellent Johan Cruyff, who was at the centre of every sweeping move and who scored two goals. A few days later the Dutch beat the East Germans 2-0, and with Brazil also having won their two games – albeit less convincingly than Holland – the clash between the Europeans and the South Americans would decide who went into the final.

Unfortunately, what should have been a classic turned out to be a very sordid affair. From the first World Cup back in 1930, teams from Brazil had been noted for their soccer skills. Thus, it saddened fans to see the Brazilians casting aside their usual flowing football, and instead resort to tough tackling and rough-house methods against the Dutch – who, it must be said, retaliated in kind.

If there were no goals scored in the first half, it did not mean that the game was without incident. Dutchman Neeskens had been knocked out by the robust defender Marinho. After the interval, when the irrepressible Neeskens was cut down ruthlessly in a tackle by Periera, the referee had no option but to send off the Brazilian defender. Reduced to ten men, the world champions fought valiantly to keep their crown, but Neeskens coolly lobbed Brazilian goalie Leao for the first goal, and the ever-vigilant Cruyff crashed home a second goal from a cross by winger Krol.

Holland were in their first-ever World Cup final and in the next few days, thousands more of their supporters joined the fans already in West Germany, confident of seeing their team being crowned champions.

A tide of euphoria swept across Holland and such was the mood of the moment that the government gave permission for a special stamp to be printed, proclaiming the national side world champions. Tens of thousands of stamps were turned out, ready to go on sale after Holland had won the final.

The confidence of the Dutch was not misplaced. In Group B the favourites, West Germany, struggled in their first game against Yugoslavia but eventually ran out 2-0 winners. What was significant was that Beckenbauer was the outstanding player on the park. In the second game against Sweden, the Germans were 0-1 behind at half-time, but scored four goals in the second half and eventually ran out 4-2 winners.

The impressive Poles had also won their two games, so the crunch tie with West Germany in Frankfurt would decide who would qualify to meet Holland in the final. A rainstorm delayed the kick-off and made the pitch almost unplayable. The rain also probably washed away any chances the elegant Poles had of beating their well-drilled opponents. The stronger West Germans were always in command and it was no surprise when, late in the second half, Gerd Muller, nicknamed 'The Bomber' for his goal-scoring ability, blasted the only goal of the game past Tomaszewski, the Polish custodian, who had earlier saved a penalty.

So it was West Germany versus their deadly rivals and near neighbours Holland in the World Cup final. For the fans of the two nations who packed into the stadium in Munich, it meant something else – a duel between Cruyff and Beckenbauer, the two best players in the world. It would surely be a soccer classic.

The final was indeed a cracker – and it got off to an amazing start when Holland scored in the opening seconds without a West German player touching the ball! It was Cruyff who was the instigator of the golden goal.

Straight from the kick-off, the Dutch began to stroke the ball arrogantly from man to man. When the ball was played forward, Cruyff, who had anticipated the pass, controlled the ball brilliantly, sprinted into the German penalty area and, turning past his marker, Berti Vogts, was tripped by a despairing tackle from Hoeness. A concerted roar of outrage went forth from the thousands of Dutch fans on the terraces and the referee had no hesitation in pointing to the penalty spot.

Johan Neeskens strode forward and smacked the spot kick past Maier in the German goal. 1-0 to Holland. It was the most sensational start ever to a World Cup final.

For the next 25 minutes the Dutch toyed with the West Germans. The Dutch fans roared their approval as precision passes from their heroes unerringly found a team-mate and it looked only a matter of time before Holland would score again. Helmut Schoen, the wily West German manager, had given the indefatigable Vogts the unenviable task of marking Cruyff and in that opening period the little blond midfielder was struggling. Beckenbauer was having a quiet game.

Unfortunately, for all their classic play, the Dutch did not press home their advantage. And suddenly the Germans, initially stunned by that quick goal, began to grow in confidence and come more into the game. Urged on by their supporters, they began to attack the always-suspect Dutch defence. In midfield, Berti Vogts was tightening his hold on Johan Cruyff.

In the thirty-eighth minute West Germany equalised – and again the goal was scored from the penalty spot. Winger Holzenbein was weaving his way through a hesitant Dutch defence when Jensen tripped him. Full-back Breitner scored from the penalty and the West Germans were level. Johnny Rep had a great chance to score again for Holland after a cunning pass from Cruyff, but he fluffed it. Both teams strove for the decisive breakthrough.

It was the West Germans who got it just before half-time, and it was ace goal-scorer Gerd Muller who sent the home fans ecstatic when he took a pass from Bonhof, pulled the ball back with one foot and nonchalantly swept it past Jongbloed with the other. The West Germans were leading 2-1 at half-time.

In the second period Holland had to bring on substitutes Van de Kerkhof and De Jong for the injured Rensenbrink and Rijsbergen and these changes disrupted the team's rhythm. That said, although Cruyff and his team-mates played some superb football and always looked dangerous anywhere within 30 yards of goal, the West Germans, with Beckenbauer now a masterful figure in midfield, were more workmanlike and solid.

There were quite a few goalmouth incidents in the second half, but Holland, for all their brilliance, just could not score that elusive goal that would tie the game. Indeed, it was goal-poacher Muller who scored again for West Germany, but the goal was disallowed for a doubtful offside decision.

Not long after English referee Jack Taylor had blown the final whistle, the disconsolate Johann Cruyff and his Dutch team watched as Beckenbauer and his colleagues went up to receive the trophy. For Cruyff it was a particularly bitter moment; his one and only appearance in a World Cup final had ended in failure.

Final

West Germany 2	**Holland 1**
Breitner (penalty)	Neeskens (penalty)
Muller	

Half-time 2-1

· ARGENTINA ·

THE long, lean figure of one man dominated the 1978 World Cup, held in Argentina against strong opposition from other nations, due to the fact that it was a country ruled by a military dictatorship. Cesar Luis Menotti was the Argentinian manager, charged with winning the coveted trophy for the first time for the soccer-mad host country.

His fellow countrymen nicknamed him El Flaco (The Thin One). He was a tall, doleful-looking man with long, lank hair and a cigarette perpetually between his lips. The Argentinians' participation in the World Cup had, over the years, been noted more for their rough play than for their skilful football.

Memories of the disgraceful Argentinian performance against England in the 1966 tournament, when it took the referee eight minutes to get centre-half Antonio Rattin off the field after a series of vicious fouls, were still fresh in many people's minds.

Argentinian fans were noted for their volatile behaviour at soccer games, and that violence was matched in no small measure by the players themselves. It was felt that Argentina would go to any lengths to win the World Cup in front of their own fans. Cesar Menotti, a former player, knew his country had a bad reputation and had vowed to win the World Cup by pure skill alone.

It was a tall order. Argentina was in the grip of General George Videla's military junta. Thousands of people, opponents of the regime, had mysteriously disappeared, never to be seen again. Murders and assassinations were an everyday occurrence. A bomb had been found in the press centre in Buenos Aires a few weeks before the tournament began, killing a policeman when it was being taken away. Violence was in the air and it needed little to spark and start off a riot.

Argentina badly needed a success of international importance, and winning the World Cup would go a long way towards restoring esteem. The military poured a huge amount of money, which the country could not afford, into the staging of the World Cup and they expected Menotti to deliver.

Sensing the atmosphere of menace, some countries were reluctant to send teams to Argentina. They feared for the safety of their players, believing that referees would be intimidated by the fiery home crowds. As it turned out, those fears were not unfounded.

Meanwhile, Menotti was minus several of his star players who were playing in Europe and who were not released by their Spanish and Italian clubs. Fortunately, he did have the services of Mario Kempes, a great goal grabber, who was released for World Cup duty by Valencia in Spain. Menotti would pair him up front with the dangerous Leopoldo Luque as a double-pronged strike force. In midfield he had a little dynamo called Osvaldo Ardiles, later to play for and manage Tottenham Hotspur and Swindon Town in England. Attack was Menotti's motto – but would it pay off?

Argentina were drawn in Group 1 against three of Europe's top teams – Hungary, Italy and France. When the team took the field in their first game against Hungary, the packed River Plate Stadium burst forth with nationalistic fervour. The atmosphere was intimidating and it was no surprise when Portuguese referee

Garrido sent off two Hungarians for fouling near the end, although by then the host country was leading 2-1, which was to be the final score.

A few days later when Argentina beat the classy French team, again by 2-1, the victory was helped by one-sided refereeing, this time by Switzerland's Monsieur Dubach. He awarded a dubious penalty to Argentina in the dying seconds of the first half, from which Passarella duly scored. France equalised early in the second half, but fell behind to a thundering shot by Luque on the half-hour. With ten minutes remaining, French forward Didier Six was blatantly pulled down by an Argentinian defender in the penalty area, but the referee waved play on.

Once again the whole of Argentina went wild. Fireworks exploded in the streets, and in bars and cafés in every town and city crowds of people sang and danced. Cesar Menotti and his footballing caballeros were becoming national heroes. Pictures of the mournful, chain-smoking Menotti appeared in newspapers and on television screens around the world. But El Flaco knew that his team would need every bit of good fortune, and some help from officialdom, if it was to win the World Cup.

National fervour was dampened when Argentina played Italy in the final game of Group 1. Both teams had already qualified for the quarter-finals, but whichever team won would stay in Buenos Aires, while the losers would play in Rosario in the next round. Italy won 1-0 and for the first time Menotti came in for criticism.

The Argentinian manager enjoyed a slice of luck when, in the quarter-finals, his team was drawn in the 'easy' group with deadly rivals Brazil, Poland and Peru. The other, much tougher grouping consisted of Italy, Holland, West Germany and Austria, with any of the first three capable of lifting the World Cup. Menotti reckoned that only Brazil stood in the way of Argentina reaching the final.

Argentina defeated Poland 2-0 in their first match in the group, while Brazil beat Peru 3-0. The two long-time rivals clashed in the next game, a bruising 0-0 encounter, more noted for Menotti's consumption of cigarettes than for the quality of the football. This left Brazil with a vital goal difference advantage over Argentina and everything now depended on the last two games, Brazil versus Poland and Argentina against Peru, to see which team would reach the World Cup final.

Once again officialdom weighed in on Argentina's side. Instead of the two games being played simultaneously, Brazil were ordered to play Poland in the afternoon, with Argentina taking on Peru in the evening. It was a blatant bit of favouritism which would leave Argentina knowing exactly what they would have to do against Peru to reach the final. Brazilian officials protested at this disgraceful arrangement, but to no avail.

Brazil defeated Poland by 3-1. This meant that the home side would have to beat Peru by four clear goals to reach the World Cup final. In goal for the Peruvians was Quinoga, reckoned by many to be the best goalkeeper in the tournament.

Life in Argentina came to a standstill as the kick-off approached. The country was in ferment and bars and cafés across the country were packed to capacity. When Menotti's men took the field, they did so to a thunderous roar of encouragement from the crowd as tons of shredded paper fluttered in the floodlights. Fireworks exploded and the tension reverberated around the stadium.

Was that the reason for Peru's collapse that night? Six goals crashed past the helpless Quinoga as Kempes & Co. ran riot. Twice in the first few minutes Peru almost scored, but after that early spurt, the fight went out of the team and they succumbed far too easily for some people's liking. For the home side, centre-forward Kempes, who scorerd two goals, was in sparkling form. The result, however, and the manner in which it was achieved, left a sour taste in many mouths.

Claudio Coutinho, Brazil's outraged manager, accused the Argentinians of 'fixing' the game with the Peruvians. The Argentinians counter-charged and alleged that Brazil had offered the Peruvians money to play well. Coutinho said the players of Peru could never again be proud to hear their country's national anthem. The Peruvian goalkeeper published an open letter in which he tried to defend his team's performance. Members of the Dutch team, whom Argentina would meet in the final, were in no doubt that skulduggery had taken place. Others felt that the Argentinians had been simply brilliant on the night.

One man, Cesar Luis Menotti, smoked cigarettes and took the criticism in his stride. He had promised that his team would play open football and score goals. What was everyone complaining about? His thoughts were on the final against Holland.

True to form, it was an ill-tempered World Cup final, which did not reflect credit on either team. The Argentinians purposely came onto the field five minutes late and immediately began niggling, protesting about an innocuous bandage which Dutch winger Van de Kerkhof was wearing on an injured forearm. The referee refused to start the game until the bandage had been changed.

The packed stadium was a sea of blue and white Argentinian flags, with the fans screaming their support – an intimidating atmosphere for any referee. Amidst it all, Cesar Luis Menotti sat smoking impassively on the bench. For him, the moment of truth had arrived.

Seven minutes before half-time of an evenly contested encounter came the goal all Argentina was waiting for: a swift interchange of passes on the left side of the field and forward Luque slipped the ball to his partner, Kempes. The latter swung his deadly left foot and Jongbloed in the Dutch goal was beaten. 1-0 to Argentina.

Holland pressed forward in the second half and got the equaliser they deserved when the tall Dirk Nanninga, brought on to trouble the Argentinian defence in the air, rose to head past Fillol. It was still even up to the last minute when a shot from Dutch forward Rob Rensenbrink hit the post and went wide, to the groans of the Dutch fans. El Flaco's face showed no emotion, but he knew it had been a close shave.

Extra time. Which team would last the pace? The Argentinians, spurred on by their fanatical supporters, took the lead again in the last minute of the first half of extra-time through Kempes, who held off several tackles to slip the ball past Jongbloed. After the change-over, the Dutch threw caution to the wind and poured forward in attack, leaving gaps in their defence. With five minutes of play remaining, the Argentinians scored again through winger Bertoni to make it 3-1. The final whistle set off scenes of emotion in which even Menotti got involved.

His gamble to get his team playing total football had paid off. A non-conformist where tactics were concerned, taciturn and unemotional, Menotti won the World Cup for his country, but never became a folk hero. To this day El Flaco must wonder what would have been his fate had that effort from Rensenbrink gone into the net instead of hitting the upright. His team had survived a last-minute scare to win the World Cup by the width of a goalpost.

Final

Argentina 3	**Holland 1**
Kempes (2)	Nanninga
Bertoni	

(after extra-time)

Half-time 1-0 ***Full Time 1-1***

· SPAIN ·

THIS was the World Cup that spread its wings into Africa and Asia and for which twenty-four nations, instead of the usual contingent of sixteen, qualified for the finals for the first time. Chief proponent for the move to expand was the Brazilian-born president of FIFA, Joao Havelange, who had made it one of his election pledges when campaigning for the office.

When Frenchmen Jules Rimet, who was president of FIFA from 1920 to 1954, and his compatriot Henri Delaunay had first conceived the idea of a world tournament for soccer nations, they had wanted it to encompass the globe. Now that aim had been achieved by Havelange. While the move was welcomed by the emerging soccer nations in Africa and Asia, it made for a top-heavy tournament, with the teams being split into six groups of four, played on a round robin basis. Thus, the first round alone necessitated thirty-six matches being contested.

In all, including the final and the game between the two losing semi-finalists to decide third and fourth places, a further sixteen games were played. Weary players had to contend not only with injury problems, but with a Spanish heatwave which was at its worst during the month of the World Cup. There were several reported cases of players suffering from sunburn and dehydration during matches, and at the interval in many of the games, team members swathed themselves in cold towels in the dressing-room.

Argentina came to Spain as world champions, determined to retain the title they had won four years previously on their own soil. Cesar Luis Menotti, the chain-smoking manager who had guided the Argentinians to that memorable victory, was still in charge, and they also had free-scoring attacker Mario Kempes, the tough tackling captain and centre-back Daniel Passarella, and the inventive midfielder, Ossie Ardiles, from the previous campaign.

But the star of the team was undoubtedly 21-year-old Diego Maradona, making his World Cup debut for Argentina and reckoned to be the player of the tournament. Thick-set, agile, with uncanny ball control allied to a sharp football brain, the former street urchin was the target for opposing defenders. Unfortunately, Maradona was fouled so repeatedly during the tournament that he would eventually retaliate and suffer the indignity of being sent to the bench.

One of the big surprises in the first round of the tournament was the poor form of Italy, and also Spain, the host nation. Italy, thanks to three lacklustre drawn games, scraped into the second round from Group 1. The twelve teams who qualified were then split into four groups of three, with the winners of each group qualifying for the semi-final. When Italy were drawn in Group C with Brazil and Argentina, it looked odds on that they would be eliminated.

In Group 5 Spain had suffered the humiliation of being beaten by Northern Ireland in front of their own supporters in Valencia. The Irish had to overcome not only the intense heat, but also some very tough tackling from the Spaniards which the Paraguayan referee chose to ignore. The battling Irish never lost their composure, however, and stunned the packed stadium two minutes into the second half when centre-forward Billy Hamilton shot, goalkeeper Arconada blocked but could not hold the ball, and Gerry

Armstrong banged it into the net. The Spanish crowd roared their team on and the level of excitement matched the temperature. Referee Ortiz sent off Irish defender Mal Donaghy for a trivial misdemeanour with fifteen minutes remaining.

Despite this, Northern Ireland held on for a famous 1-0 victory. Thanks, however, to a couple of borderline penalty decisions in their other games against Honduras and Yugoslavia – it was imperative for the financial success of the tournament that the host country advance – Spain struggled into the second round, where they were paired in Group B with West Germany and England.

Here, there was no escape for the Spaniards. Despite fanatical support from the masses in the Bernabeu Stadium in Madrid they went down 2-1 to the very competitive West Germans. The latter then played a drawn game with England, and when Spain and England could only draw their game, they were both eliminated and West Germany advanced to the semi-finals.

Italy, incredibly, began to show vast improvement from their first round games. With centre-forward Paolo Rossi emerging from the shadow of an alleged soccer-fixing scandal in Italy and lucky to be in the squad, at last finding his scoring form they began to win games. Rossi did not score in Italy's 2-1 defeat of Argentina; the unlikely hero of that vicious encounter in Barcelona was midfielder Claudio Gentile, the defender who used fair means and foul to stop wonder-boy Diego Maradona from playing his usual star role. Time and time again throughout the game, Gentile's thundering tackles left Maradona shaking his head ruefully and hobbling away.

A few days later Brazil beat Argentina 3-1 in a torrid encounter in Barcelona, with Maradona being sent off for kicking his marker in frustration with five minutes to go. By then Brazil were 3-0 in front. So the World Cup holders were out and the semi-final place rested between Italy and Brazil, a vital game which Italy won by 3-2 in Barcelona.

Just how inconsistent the standard of refereeing was in Spain was demonstrated a few days later when West Germany met France in the other semi-final in Seville. The game has become synonymous with the infamous foul perpetrated by the German goalkeeper Harald Schumacher on the French forward Patrick Battison early in the second half when the score was 1-1.

With a place in the final at stake, the tension was at fever pitch. Battison had just come on as a replacement for his team-mate Genghini when he raced clear down the middle after a through ball which had split the German defence. Battison beat the giant Schumacher in the race for the ball, but the German goalkeeper committed the ultimate foul, raising his forearm and smashing it into the Frenchman's face.

Millions of television viewers around the world saw Battison lying inert on the turf, before being stretchered off to hospital with severe concussion and two missing teeth. To everyone's astonishment, no penalty was given and Schumacher was not even sent off. The game finished 1-1 and went into extra-time. The French looked to be into the final when they were leading 3-1 at one stage, but Rummenigge and centre-forward Fischer got two goals back for the resilient Germans in the second period of extra-time and it was down to penalties, five to be taken by each side.

In a tense penalty shoot-out, Stielike was the first to miss for Germany. Schumacher saved the spot kicks of Didier Six and Maxime Bossis and the tally was 4-3 in favour of West Germany who, after an epic encounter, were through to the final. The foul by Schumacher on Battison made it a most unpopular victory for the Germans.

In the other semi-final Paolo Rossi, the man who had come to Spain under a cloud, was about to become the darling of the fervent Italian press. Poland was the team which was standing between Italy and a place in the final, and even without their star forward Zbigniew Boniek, who was under suspension, they were expected to be too good for an Italian team which had still to show its true form.

The real difference between the two teams was the waif-like Rossi. He skipped over sliding tackles from the Polish defenders, got into excellent scoring positions and was always threatening the Polish defence. Halfway through the first half of a rugged encounter, he cleverly sliced the ball past Mylnarczyk in the Polish goal after it had been driven into the penalty area from a free kick by team-mate Antognoni.

Halfway through the second half, Rossi sent the huge Italian contingent in the Nou Camp stadium delirious when he scored his second goal. This time he came from nowhere between a packed Polish defence to meet a cross from little winger Bruno Conti and headed the ball into the Polish net. It was a spectacular goal and the stadium became a sea of blue and white Italian flags.

The clash of the Italians and the West Germans in the final in Madrid's Bernabeu Stadium was truly a meeting of the giants. As a football spectacle, however, it was singularly lacking in style, grace and excitement. The flow of the game was continually interrupted as both teams committed a succession of ill-tempered fouls, with Italy's hard man Claudio Gentile going perilously close to being sent off after a succession of fouls on Germany's flying winger Pierre Littbarski.

German coach Jupp Derwall had ignored grumbles from some of his players and gambled by playing star forward Karl-Heinz Rummenigge, still not fully fit, in the final. The blond Rummenigge, Europe's Footballer of the Year, would struggle to make an impression in this rugged encounter. With so much hard tackling and body checking in evidence, defenders, on both teams went close to giving away a penalty. Halfway through the first half, giant German defender Briegel lunged at little Italian winger Conti and a spot-kick was given. Full-back Cabrini, however, sent his shot wide of Schumacher's right-hand post and the half ended scoreless.

Once again it was Paolo Rossi, the little centre-forward whose place in the squad had been in doubt for so long, who broke the deadlock. Eleven minutes into the second half he stole in behind the German defence to head a cross from Gentile past Schumacher. Twelve minutes later and Rossi was the instigator of the second Italian goal, engaging in a neat exchange of passes before releasing midfielder Tardelli, who smashed the ball into the German net. At 2-0 up, the Italians were rampant, their fans delirious. A minute later Rummenigge hobbled off and was substituted by Muller.

Any chance the Germans had of saving the game disappeared with ten minutes to go when the Italians moved the ball quickly out of defence to Conti. The little winger scampered 40 yards, pulled the ball across the German goal to the tall Altobelli. He coolly picked his spot and slid it past Schumacher. 3-0 to Italy.

The Germans got a consolation goal in the dying minutes through Paul Breitner, but at the end they were a well-beaten team. Italy had won their third World Cup and West Germany had lost for the first time in the final. And the young Diego Maradona? He would make his mark in no uncertain manner when the finals were held four years later in Mexico.

Final

Italy 3	**West Germany 1**
Rossi	Breitner
Tardelli	
Altobelli	

Half-time 0-0

· MEXICO ·

HIS name was on the lips of everyone at the World Cup in Mexico in 1986. Even before the tournament began, Diego Maradona, the former Argentinian youngster who had played his early soccer in backstreets but whose footballing talents had rocketted him to millionaire status, was making headlines.

And when it was all over and victors and vanquished had departed the scene, fresh controversy raged around the head, or rather the hand, of Maradona. The 'Hand of God' goal he scored against England in the Azteca Stadium in Mexico City has gone into the annals of soccer history as one of the most bizarre incidents of all time.

Even before a ball was kicked, however, controversy had arisen about where the World Cup was going to be staged. Originally, Colombia was the favourite to host the soccer carnival, but amid charges of favouritism, the Brazilian-born president of FIFA, Joao Havelange, had thrown his considerable weight behind Mexico. Thus, despite the fact that only sixteen years earlier that country had hosted the tournament, and that the intense heat and games being played at high altitude had posed considerable problems for players, Havelange had his way.

The European teams baulked at the prospect of competing in

Mexico City at an altitude of 7,400 feet. They feared that since it was not a prosperous country, the designated stadia might not meet the required standard.

The protests were of no avail. Colombia was by-passed and Mexico won the day. Not even an earthquake which hit the country and did millions of pesos' worth of damage less than a year before the World Cup was due to kick off, could change Havelange's mind.

Mexico had never won the World Cup – indeed over the years it had one of the worst records of any nation in the tournament. Mexico's soccer-mad followers saw the stroke of good fortune of playing at home in front of fanatical support as a chance to do well, and maybe even win the coveted trophy.

The twenty-four teams which had qualified for the finals were split into six groups of four. Mexico were drawn in Group B and they set the country alight when they beat Belgium by 2-1 in their first game. A 1-1 draw with Paraguay, followed by a 1-0 win over Iraq saw the Mexicans top their group and qualify for the next round.

When Mexico beat Bulgaria by 2-0 before a full house in the Azteca Stadium in Mexico City to qualify for the last eight, the nation went wild. Such were the unprecedented scenes in the capital that four people were shot dead in the night-long revelry, and hundreds of people needed hospital treatment after being involved in traffic accidents.

Three days later when Mexico met West Germany in Monterey for a place in the semi-finals, the country came to a standstill. Unfortunately, that was where the dream ended. The solid Germans held the Mexicans to a scoreless draw, they won the tense penalty shoot-out by 4-1. Mexico went into mourning.

National fervour apart, it was the Argentinian/England quarter-final clash that really caught the attention of the soccer world.

Four years earlier, the two countries had fought a bitter and bloody war over the Falkland Islands. England had come out on top on that occasion, and when fate decreed that the two countries face each other in the World Cup, it was inevitable that this occasion would have its quota of drama. Nobody, however, could have anticipated just how dramatic this confrontation would be.

Unfortunately for such a tense encounter, the organising committee took the inexplicable decision of putting a relatively inexperienced referee, Tunisian Ali Ben Naceur, in charge.

Before the game, England manager Bobby Robson told journalists that 'without Diego Maradona, Argentina's chance of winning the World Cup would be practically nil.' Robson was proved right in the most amazing fashion in the 50th minute in the Azteca Stadium when Maradona scored his infamous 'Hand of God' goal, one of the most controversial goals in the history of the World Cup.

The game had been evenly balanced up to then, with no score at half-time. Five minutes into the second half, England defender Steve Hodge, under pressure, hooked the ball over his head for goalkeeper Peter Shilton to advance and collect. Maradona was lurking, however, rose in the air with Shilton and flicked the ball into the net, not with his head, but with his hand! To everyone's amazement the referee pointed to the centre-spot. He was awarding a goal!

Maradona was smiling broadly as he was congratulated by ecstatic team-mates. Meanwhile England goalkeeper Shilton, dumbfounded at first, lead a charge as outraged members of the English team protested to referee Naceur. It was all to no avail; neither of the linesmen objected to the goal and Mr Naceur allowed it to stand.

The crowd had barely time to recover from that incident when, four minutes later, Maradona rubbed salt into England's wound by scoring a goal of stunning quality. And this time it was legitimate. Receiving the ball in the Argentinian half, Maradona set off on an amazing solo effort that brought the crowd to its feet. Swerving, feinting, riding tackles, Diego beat six English defenders before sliding the ball into the net past Shilton.

England were still two goals down well into the second half when substitute winger John Barnes sent over a cross which centre-forward Gary Lineker headed past Pumpido in the Argentinian goal. England almost pulled the game out of the fire with four minutes to go in a repeat move, but this time Lineker just failed to connect with the ball.

At the final whistle, anger and frustration escalated both on the terraces and in the English dressing-room. Mexican riot police had to move in quickly to quell clashes between British and Argentinian fans who seemed set to wage the Falklands war all over again. Fortunately, the pockets of disturbance were eventually dampened down.

Not so the torrent of abuse in the English dressing-room directed towards the referee and Diego Maradona. An angry Bobby Robson described the first goal as a diabolical decision. Peter Shilton, the English captain, was even more forthright: he described the goal as the worst refereeing decision he had ever seen in all his years in top-class football. 'There is no doubt that Diego Maradona cheated us out of the tournament,' said a disgusted Shilton.

Around the world television replays of the controversial goal were being transmitted and analysed, and it was plain for all to see that the referee had indeed erred. The resourceful Maradona had certainly used a part of his anatomy, other than his head, to score the goal. Confronted with the evidence, he coined the immortal phrase 'Hand of God' to explain his goal.

Whatever about divine intervention, England was out and Argentina was into the semi-finals where the team would meet the ever-improving Belgians. Once again in the Azteca Stadium the 25-year-old Maradona would show why he was already being rated the star of this World Cup. He inspired his team-mates and defied everything the Belgians did to close him down.

Putting the controversy and ill-feeling of the England game behind him, Maradona once again showed the dynamism of a great player. After a scoreless first half, he brought a rather tame encounter to life by scoring a goal with the outside of his left foot in the fiftieth minute. In the sixty-third minute he did it again, and this time it was another Maradona special. Receiving the ball with a ring of Belgian defenders around him, he jinked, dummied and swerved, beating them all in turn, before slotting the ball home. It was a goal to savour and it knocked the heart out of the Belgians.

Even before Argentina met West Germany in the final, Maradona was certain to be voted Footballer of the 1986 World Cup by the soccer writers covering the tournament. In Mexico City his name was on everybody's lips and at home he was being hailed as a hero. Diego was writing himself into soccer history, and the world awaited another dazzling display.

Surprisingly, Argentina's favourite son failed to score in his side's 3-2 victory. He did, however, frustrate his marker, Lothar Matthaus, into fouling him midway through the first half, and from the subsequent free kick, José Luis Brown opened the scoring.

Ten minutes after half-time, when Argentina went 2-0 up after Valdano scored, the writing was on the wall for West Germany. Battlers to the last, however, the West Germans staged a great comeback. Twenty-eight minutes into the half, Rummenigge scored. Eight minutes from the end the stadium went wild when substitute Rudi Voeller equalised for West Germany. Now they were the team in charge of the game.

With only six minutes to go, the score was tied and Argentina looked in danger of losing a final they had dominated. It was then that Maradona performed his last piece of magic in the tournament. Receiving the ball far out from the West German goal, he looked up and saw team-mate Burruchaga unmarked. A beautifully floated pass found its man, Burruchaga swept the ball past Schumacher in the West German goal, and the World Cup was Argentina's for a second time.

If Maradona was disappointed not to score in the final, he did not say so to the horde of reporters who besieged him afterwards. One soccer scribe was heard to remark jocosely that keeping Diego Maradona scoreless on the day was probably the Almighty's revenge, having been blamed for scoring that controversial goal against England!

Final

Argentina 3	**West Germany 2**
Brown	Rummenigge
Valdano	Voeller
Burruchaga	

Half-time 1-0

IN 1990 the World Cup returned to Italian soil for only the second time, fifty-six years after it had first been held there in 1934. In the intervening years, huge technological advances had been made in communications, stadia design and football technique. Sadly, only the first two were in evidence in Italy; the standard of football on display throughout the finals was eminently forgettable, with the final in Rome between old rivals Argentina and West Germany probably the worst ever.

Four years previously in Mexico, those two teams had clashed in the World Cup final, with Argentina winning by a 3-2 margin. On that occasion, the football had been far from vintage, but at least the fans had the consolation of seeing the two teams scoring five goals, with West Germany making a spirited fight back after being two goals down.

In Rome's Olympic stadium, everything that went wrong with the modern game was seen by a television audience of millions. Two teams, boasting players of consummate skill like Maradona, Burruchaga, Matthaus and Voeller, threw their skills to the wind and instead resorted to negative, ill-tempered and downright dirty play. At the final whistle, West Germany had won by a goal to nil, scored from a penalty which many felt should not have been awarded.

Those from another era watching the game and seeing the spoiling tactics, interspersed with a litany of fouls, must have longed for the free-flowing football of yesteryear. It was a World Cup final that left a bad taste in the mouth and, with luck, will never be repeated.

Yet the tournament had started so promisingly, with the opening match of the tournament providing a sensational upset when the unheralded team from Cameroon defeated world champions Argentina in Group B. Cameroon's 1-0 victory in Milan's San Siro Stadium was a result that sent shock waves to the European and South American teams who had dominated the World Cup since its inception in 1930.

From the 1980s teams from Africa, benefiting from top-class coaching from Europe and South America, and with abundant talent at their disposal, Cameroon had improved immeasurably in technique. Results since then had shown that teams from Africa were no longer the pushovers of former years.

Still, Argentina were world champions and came to Italy confident of retaining that title. Cesar Luis Menotti, the chain-smoking manager whose total football approach had bathed Argentina in World Cup glory in 1978, was long gone. In charge now was former player Dr Carlos Bilardo, much criticised within his own country, but who nevertheless had steered Argentina to victory four years previously. Lynchpin of the side was Diego Maradona, playing his football for Napoli in Italy and making his third World Cup appearance.

Twenty-four teams had qualified for the finals in Italy, split into six groups of four from which two teams from each, plus the four best losers, would qualify for the next round. Argentina was in Group B with Romania and the Soviet Union, with

Cameroon as the rank outsider of the quartet. Nobody gave them a chance of advancing to the next round. As it turned out, Cameroon topped Group B – with the World Cup holders barely making it through as one of the best losers!

Another nation making its World Cup debut was the Republic of Ireland, managed by Jack Charlton, a bluff Geordie and an uncompromising centre-half on England's World Cup-winning team of 1966. Under Charlton, Ireland played a long ball game that was untypical of the modern era, but was one that would pay dividends in Italy. In addition, the Irish team had Jack's Army – a following of 20,000 fans who captured the hearts of the world media with their good humour and exemplary behaviour.

Ireland was drawn in Group F along with England and Holland, both favourites to advance to the next round, and rank outsiders Egypt. In the preliminary round the Irish drew 1-1 with England in rain-drenched Cagliari. This was followed by a boring 0-0 draw against Egypt in Sardinia. The Irish then had an exciting 1-1 draw with Holland to advance to the last 16. In the next round against Romania the battling Irish drew 0-0. When extra time failed to produce another score, the game went to a tense penalty shoot-out.

It was later recorded that the Irish Prime Minister Charles Haughey left a European Community meeting in Dublin to witness that penalty shoot-out. And when Irish goalkeeper Packie Bonner saved Timofte's final penalty of five for Romania, and centre-half Dave O'Leary scored his final one to put Ireland unexpectedly through to the quarter-final, it sparked off an Irish party that lasted for days!

In veteran Roger Milla, Cameroon had the outstanding character, if not the best player, of the tournament. Aged 38 (some said he was 40), he had played all his football in France before retiring to play part-time nearer home. Such was his form on the island of Réunion that he was picked for the Cameroon team at the behest of the country's President.

He would never play a full game in Italy, being brought on in the second half of games to add firepower to the Cameroon forward line. Milla the Magnificent would leave his stamp on the 1990 World Cup, overshadowing even the great Maradona.

Against Argentina he was on for a mere eight minutes. By then the tough-tackling, speedy Africans were one goal up and were playing with only ten men, defender Kana Biyik having been sent off for a dangerous tackle in the sixty-second minute. Undeterred, the men from Cameroon scored the only goal of the game five minutes later, and when Milla was brought on he infused new life into the team. Dejected Argentinian manager Carlos Bilardo described the defeat as the worst of his career.

In their next game, in Bari, Cameroon caused another upset by beating Romania 2-1, both goals being scored by Roger Milla. This time the sprightly veteran was brought on thirteen minutes into the second half with his team struggling to find the Romanian net. Roger soon showed them how! Back home he was now a hero. The Cameroon President ordained that Roger Milla be brought on at some stage in every game.

He was brought on in the first half in the final group match against the Soviet Union. By then Cameroon were assured of going into the next round and they treated their defeat by 4-0 as a mere training spin.

Meanwhile, hosts Italy had also found an unlikely hero in Salvatore 'Toto' Schillaci, the Sicilian-born centre-forward, who had fought his way up from poverty to play for glamour side Juventus, but who, like Milla, had been included in the Italian squad only as a substitute. In the World Cup, pint-sized Schillaci seized his chance when the elegant Gianluca Vialli was injured early on. 'Toto' Schillaci's goal-grabbing qualities would make him the hero of Italy.

These two men, Milla, tall and explosive, Schillaci, small and slippery, would overshadow bigger names like Maradona and Matthaus of West Germany. Sadly neither Milla nor Schillaci would play in the final, but the two would be remembered long after this World Cup was forgotten.

Both continued their goal-scoring feats in the second round of the tournament. Milla the Magnificent did just that in Cameroon's game against Colombia in Naples. Once again he was brought on early in the second half of the game when neither side had scored and the match was hanging delicately in the balance. It was still 0-0 at the final whistle, but in the second half of extra-time Milla exploded into action, beating two men and cracking the ball past Colombian goalkeeper Higuita.

A couple of minutes later the flamboyant Higuita advanced 40 yards from his goal with the ball and tried to dribble past Milla, who dispossessed him. The sprightly Roger, belying his age, dashed downfield with the ball and stroked it into the empty Colombian net. Cameroon were through to the last eight, where they would meet mighty England.

In Italy's second round match in Rome against Uruguay, Schillaci was preferred to the fit-again Vialli. He repaid manager Azeglio Vicini's confidence by scoring a goal in the 2-0 defeat of the Uruguayans. Soccer crazy Italian fans danced in the streets, chanting 'Toto', 'Toto'.

The little Sicilian did it again a few nights later in Rome in a torrid game against the Republic of Ireland. The 20,000 Irish fans in the Olympic Stadium cheered and sang themselves hoarse through the game, but Schillaci ended the Irish dream late in the first half when he scored, after Bonner in the Irish goal could only block a hard shot from midfielder Donadoni. Schillaci cracked the ball home for the only goal of the game. He was unlucky in the second half when he again put the ball into the Irish net only to be ruled offside.

In Naples, Cameroon's dream of reaching the finals died – but it took two goals from penalties and for the match to go to extra-time before England got through 3-2. Once again it was that man Milla, making his usual early second-half appearance, who inspired Cameroon. Up to then they were trailing 1-0 to a David Platt goal. Milla began his magic and Paul Gascoigne upended him in the penalty area. Centre-back Kunde scored from the spot kick and three minutes later Cameroon were ahead when Milla gave a delightful pass to Ekeke, who beat Peter Shilton in the English goal.

Leading 2-1, Cameroon were within eight minutes of a semi-final place with Roger Milla, the oldest man ever to score in a World Cup tournament, playing the game of his life. But, whereas the Africans in their green shirts were tiring and beginning to look ragged, the English players were still full of running. The scene was set for a dramatic ending.

In the eighty-second minute, England's centre-forward Gary Lineker was brought down in the penalty area. His spot kick made the score 2-2. Into extra-time and another penalty to England. Again it was Lineker who was brought down, this time by goalkeeper N'Kono. Lineker scored and England advanced to meet West Germany in the semi-final. The men from Cameroon went home empty-handed, but bathed in glory.

Italy's dream of repeating the 1934 World Cup win before their own supporters died in Naples when, after a 1-1 draw against Argentina, they lost 4-3 in the penalty shoot-out. The other semi-final between West Germany and England in Turin also ended 1-1 and it too was decided on penalties. The Germans missed one of their five, but Stuart Pearce and Chris Waddle failed to convert theirs for England. This meant that West Germany was in the final on a 4-3 penalty count.

In contrast to the excitement engendered by teams like Cameroon, and to a lesser extent by Italy and England, the final played in the magnificent Olympic Stadium in Rome did not live up to the occasion. A fit Diego Maradona would have been expected to weave his magic, but he had been the target of some heavy tackles from the opening game and a swollen ankle hampered him in the final.

Before the tournament began, FIFA had instructed referees to crack down on players committing a professional foul. The warning did not deter players from both teams from putting in some ferocious tackles and committing numerous petty misdemeanours. After a first half devoid of good football, the first incident of note in the second half occurred when Argentinian defender Monzon was sent off for a tackle on Germany's centre-forward Klinsmann. It left the World champions struggling to retain their title with only ten men.

Argentina held on valiantly, but with only six minutes to go, Sensini tackled Voeller in the penalty area and the German forward took a theatrical tumble. The Argentinians protested vigorously, and with some justification, when the referee pointed to the penalty spot. All to no avail. Andreas Brehme blasted the ball past Goycoechea in the Argentinian goal. The only consolation for the fans was that extra-time would not be needed to decide the drab encounter.

A team from the USA competed in the World Cup in Italy, the first time since 1950 that an American team had qualified for the finals. They lost their three games in Group A, failing by one goal to both Italy and Austria. FIFA officials were impressed by the skills of the Americans, and took the historic decision to stage the 1994 World Cup in the United States for the first time. It was a fitting tribute to a nation represented among the 13 countries which had contested the inaugural World Cup in Uruguay in 1930.

Final

West Germany 1	**Argentina 0**
Brehme (penalty)	

Half-time 0-0

· UNITED STATES ·

WHEN the 1994 World Cup in the United States kicks off officially on 17 June, with champions Germany clashing with Bolivia in the opening game in Soldiers' Field in Chicago, it will herald a new era in soccer history. Not only is the tournament being held for the first time in the US, but satellite television will bring the games to an audience estimated in billions.

The popularity of soccer around the globe today can be gauged from the fact that 145 national teams sought to qualify for the 1994 World Cup in the US. Contrast that with the inaugural World Cup tournament in 1930 when only thirteen nations sent teams to Uruguay, a mere four travelling from Europe.

Such is the appeal of today's World Cup that FIFA, the game's governing body, has divided the map of the world into six international zones in which teams undergo a long series of qualifying games from which the final 22 teams, plus the current champions and the host country, make it to the finals.

The long road to qualify for America began away back on 21 March 1992 when the Dominican Republic kicked-off against Puerto Rico in the first game in the CONCACAF (Caribbean region). That section had 23 entries from which two countries, Mexico and the United States, qualified.

The South American section, traditionally split into two zones, had nine entries, from which four nations would win through to the finals. Three times World Cup champions Brazil qualified, as did Bolivia, Colombia and Argentina. But it was only in a last-ditch play-off against Australia, winners of the Oceania section, that Argentina, World Cup finalists in 1990, made it to America.

Africa, which has experienced an explosion of soccer popularity in the past two decades, had 37 nations entered in the qualifying section of the 1994 World Cup. After an exhausting series of games, the trio to make it to the finals were Nigeria, Morocco and Cameroon. This will be Nigeria's debut in a World Cup final.

Another team making its debut in the finals is Saudi Arabia, which qualified with the Korean Republic from the Asia section. Like Africa, the Asian continent, from which 29 teams entered the qualifying stages of the 1994 World Cup, has been gripped by soccer fever in recent years. So far the Asian countries have not made the same spectacular breakthrough as the African nations.

Europe, with 38 entries plus Israel, had the largest number of teams setting out with qualification for America as their goal. With champions Germany automatically qualifying, this left the other 37 nations, split into six zones, to fight it out for the 12 places in the finals. After some nail-biting encounters, the European teams to make it to America are Greece (in its first ever finals), Russia, Norway, Sweden, Italy, Switzerland, Holland, Spain, Republic of Ireland, Romania, Belgium and Bulgaria.

The World Cup draw in the Las Vegas Convention Centre on 19 December 1993 was carried out with typical American razzmatazz and was seen by millions of soccer fans on every continent. President Clinton's appearance emphasised the importance of the occasion, as did his comment that soccer was now America's fastest-growing sport, while stars of stage, screen and television came on to extol the virtues of Los Angeles, San Francisco, Detroit, Boston, Chicago, Dallas, New York, Orlando and Washington, where first round games will be held.

FIFA general secretary Sepp Blatter acted as overseer, as well-known personalities, including former soccer greats like Bobby Charlton and Franz Beckenbauer, came onstage to pick out the little plastic balls, each containing the name of one of the competing teams, from the giant glass bowls. Soccer fans in many countries were glued to television sets to see the live satellite picture.

The host country is one of the six seeds, along with Germany, Brazil, Italy, Argentina and Belgium. Of the 24 teams that have reached this fifteenth World Cup, only four – Brazil, Argentina, Italy and West Germany – have won the trophy since it was inaugurated (neither Uruguay, who have won it twice, nor England, winners in 1966, have qualified this time).

Can the United States upset the odds and lift the trophy in front of their own fans next July? No doubt they will put up a good show, but the most likely result is for either Germany, Brazil or Italy to become World Cup champions for a record fourth time.

As soccer enters the satellite era, the ghosts of Jules Rimet and Henri Delaunay, the two Frenchmen who began it all back in 1930, must have smiled benignly and marvelled at the excitement and high-tech proceedings in the Las Vegas Convention Centre. It was all so different when they set out to bring the soccer nations of the world together in friendly combat.

What was once a dream is now a reality and is perhaps best encapsulated in the two World Cup posters which link the generations. FIFA's 1930 poster for the Uruguayan finals depicts the figure of a goalkeeper at full stretch saving a shot. For the

1994 World Cup, Peter Max, one of America's foremost artists, has designed a poster showing a footballer kicking a ball from earth into space. 'It represents,' he says, 'the universal appeal of the sport.'

THE WORL

GROUP A
(1) USA
(2) SWITZERLAND
(3) COLOMBIA
(4) ROMANIA

GROUP B
(1) BRAZIL
(2) RUSSIA
(3) CAMEROON
(4) SWEDEN

GROUP C
(1) GERMANY
(2) BOLIVIA
(3) SPAIN
(4) SOUTH KOREA

LOS ANGELES		
Sat June 18	A3 v A4	COLOMBIA ROMANIA
Sun June 19	B3 v B4	CAMEROON SWEDEN
Wed June 22	A1 v A3	U.S.A. COLOMBIA
Sun June 26	A1 v A4	U.S.A. ROMANIA

CHICAGO		
Fri June 17	C1 v C2	GERMANY BOLIVIA
Tues June 21	C1 v C3	GERMANY SPAIN
Sun June 26	D4 v D2	BULGARIA GREECE
Mon June 27	C2 v C3	BOLIVIA SPAIN

BOSTON		
Tues June 21	D1 v D2	ARGENTINA GREECE
Thur June 23	C4 v C2	SOUTH KOREA BOLIVIA
Sat June 25	D1 v D3	ARGENTINA NIGERIA
Thur June 30	D2 v D3	GREECE NIGERIA

ORLANDO		
Sun June 19	F1 v F2	BELGIUM MOROCCO
Fri June 24	E4 v E2	MEXICO IRELAND
Sat June 25	F1 v F3	BELGIUM HOLLAND
Wed June 29	F2 v F3	MOROCCO HOLLAND

WASHINGTON		
Sun June 19	E3 v E4	NORWAY MEXICO
Mon June 20	F3 v F4	HOLLAND SAUDI ARABIA
Tues June 28	E1 v E4	ITALY MEXICO
Wed June 29	F1 v F4	BELGIUM SAUDI ARABIA

P DRAW 1994

GROUP D
(1) ARGENTINA
(2) GREECE
(3) NIGERIA
(4) BULGARIA

GROUP E
(1) ITALY
(2) IRELAND
(3) NORWAY
(4) MEXICO

GROUP F
(1) BELGIUM
(2) MOROCCO
(3) HOLLAND
(4) SAUDI ARABIA

NEW YORK		
Sat June 18	E1 v	**ITALY**
	E2	**IRELAND**
Thur June 23	E1 v	**ITALY**
	E3	**NORWAY**
Sat June 25	F4 v	**SAUDI ARABIA**
	F2	**MOROCCO**
Tues June 28	E2 v	**IRELAND**
	E3	**NORWAY**

SAN FRANCISCO		
Mon June 20	B1 v	**BRAZIL**
	B2	**RUSSIA**
Fri June 24	B1 v	**BRAZIL**
	B3	**CAMEROON**
Sun June 26	A2 v	**SWITZERLAND**
	A3	**COLOMBIA**
Tues June 28	B2 v	**RUSSIA**
	B3	**CAMEROON**

DETROIT		
Sat June 18	A1 v	**U.S.A.**
	A2	**SWITZERLAND**
Wed June 22	A4 v	**ROMANIA**
	A2	**SWITZERLAND**
Fri June 24	B4 v	**SWEDEN**
	B2	**RUSSIA**
Tues June 28	B1 v	**BRAZIL**
	B4	**SWEDEN**

DALLAS		
Fri June 17	C3 v	**SPAIN**
	C4	**SOUTH KOREA**
Tues June 21	D3 v	**NIGERIA**
	D4	**BULGARIA**
Mon June 27	C1 v	**GERMANY**
	C4	**SOUTH KOREA**
Thur June 30	D1 v	**ARGENTINA**
	D4	**BULGARIA**